Timesaver British History Highlights

(Pre-intermediate – Upper-intermediate)

Bill Bowler and

Lesley Thompson

SCHOLASTIC   MARY GLASGOW MAGAZINES

Introduction

History is not the past, it is a retelling of the past, and the storyteller's point of view is inevitably coloured by a) the time the story is retold; b) the place the storyteller comes from; and c) the storyteller's personal views (influenced by education, family background, and gender). The historical highlights (and dramatic lowpoints!) in this book are a modern - and hopefully balanced - British view of past events. We have included personal project suggestions so students can research and present a different side of a particular story if they want to. (The projects are perfect for a 'portfolio' approach to language teaching too!) Ignorance of another country's heritage and culture often leads to unthinking prejudice. Knowledge should bring with it more thoughtful tolerance. We hope the stories in this book help to explain why Britain and the British are like they are today!

Timesaver British History Highlights presents aspects of British history from a teenage perspective. As with all topic-based approaches, the materials provide learners with texts and activities that inform them about things they didn't know before in their own language. They also provide teachers with rewarding lessons involving minimal preparation.

ABOUT THIS BOOK

This book is divided into thirteen topics and a quiz unit. The topics are listed for easy reference on the contents pages (pages 2–3). Within each topic there are three varied sub-topic lessons at different levels.

 pre-intermediate – for students with 1–2 years of English.

 intermediate – for students with 2–3 years of English.

 upper-intermediate – for students with more than 3 years of English.

Each lesson consists of a double page of activities. The three lessons within a topic each cover a different aspect of that topic, so you can use more than one lesson with a higher level class and they will still find the material interesting. (If you choose to do this, it is best to start with lower-level lessons first, as vocabulary is recycled from one sub-topic to the next.)

The length of lessons will vary depending on the level of the class and how the material is approached. Activities can be exploited in different ways according to students' needs. Many lessons include vocabulary activation activities of different types. These can be dealt with in class. Alternatively, where class time is short, they can be set as preparatory homework. A good dictionary can help students in this case, providing opportunities for improving self-study skills. All lessons contain presentation material, which introduces the topic and gives students information about it. This is followed by activities that help students understand the text. These include matching, ordering, summary correction activities, true-false activities, gap-filling and skimming and scanning tasks. These are in most cases followed by different language practice activities. Personalised project suggestions are always included. Photocopy both pages of your chosen lesson for each student to ensure the material progresses smoothly from presentation, through reading and language work, to personalised response.

Different types of activities can be set as pairwork, group work, or whole class work. Vocabulary activation activities, language work, and project work can be set for homework. Some activities are open-ended and suitable for 'on-the-spot' discussion work. Others have specific answers. There is an answer key at the back of the book (on pages 90–96). Refer to this to check students' work as a whole class. Alternatively photocopy and distribute answers for individual or pair checking. (This is a useful technique with mixed level classes where students may sometimes be working in level-based groups using different materials.)

All the topics lead naturally into project work. The personal project suggestions can be used for 'on-the-spot' discussion work in class. After this, students can prepare projects based on other aspects of British history, or on aspects of their own culture and its history. The websites below provide useful information on British history, and by typing key words or names into a search engine, students can get more information about any topic in this book.

VOCABULARY

Vocabulary is graded by level according to the Mary Glasgow Magazines grading system. The language used is natural and appropriate for the topic and the age group. For some content-specific words students at all levels will find dictionaries or teacher input useful.

You will notice some words or phrases in each lesson are marked with an asterisk. These are words that might be beyond the level of students, that are not illustrated or explained on the page, and not guessable from context or activated in specific activities. The note *What is it in your langage?Find out!* invites students to use dictionaries to check the meaning of these asterisked words – an ideal opportunity to improve study skills. Alternatively the teacher can preteach these words, or (in a monolingual classroom) provide translation.

A number of history-specific words are recycled throughout the book, and students doing several lessons will soon become familiar with this content-specific vocabulary. There is also a list of historical time expressions at the end of this introduction.

LANGUAGE POINTS

Language content is listed in the contents pages. This is designed to help the teacher choose appropriate material for their classes.

QUIZZES AND EVALUATION

There are three two-page quizzes for each level on pages 84–89. They focus on the informational content and vocabulary presented in each topic. They are in a multiple-choice format, designed to be easy to administer and mark. The total quiz mark is out of 39 points. If you want, you can halve this to get a 50% score. The remaining 50% can be a global evaluation of students' project work, homework, and class participation. The quizzes are suitable as end-of-term or end-of-year evaluation for students who have worked through a number of topics at each level. The quiz questions are clearly divided into sections - each under a sub-topic heading. This allows teachers to adapt the quizzes easily for classes that have followed a different route through the book.

Useful Websites
about the British Royal Family:
• http://www.royal.gov.uk/output/

about UK history:
• http://en.wikipedia.org/wiki/UK_history
• http://www.luminarium.org/lumina.htm

about UK and world history:
• http://www.bbc.co.uk/history/
• http://www.schoolshistory.org.uk/
• http://www.spartacus.schoolnet.co.uk/

Historical Time Expressions

Years
1666 = sixteen sixty-six
1705 = seventeen-oh-five
1800 = eighteen hundred
1914 = nineteen fourteen
2000 = the year two thousand
2006 = two thousand and six

NOTE!
We don't say 'twenty-oh-six' for 2006.

Decades
the 1790s = the seventeen-nineties
the 1910s = the nineteen-tens
the '90s = the nineties

For someone living today,
the '90s or 'the nineties' = the 1990s

NOTE!
We don't use an apostrophe before the final 's' with decades.

Early Dates
700 BC = seven hundred B C
(before the Birth of Jesus Christ)
400 AD = four hundred A D
(after Jesus died)

NOTE!
AD is short for Anno Domini in Latin. It means 'In the Year of Our Lord'

Centuries
1500-1599 = the sixteenth century
1700s = the seventeen hundreds
the 20th century = the twentieth century
the 21st century = the twenty-first century

With centuries, we always look forward from a date to the next hundred:
1607 = the start of the seventeenth century
1350 = the middle of the fourteenth century
the 1280s = the end of the thirteenth century

Kings' and Queens' Names
For rulers we use Roman numbers:

Elizabeth I = Elizabeth the First
Elizabeth II = Elizabeth the Second
George III = George the Third
George IV = George the Fourth
George V = George the Fifth
Edward VI = Edward the Sixth
Edward VII = Edward the Seventh
Edward VIII = Edward the Eighth
Kevin IX = Kevin the Ninth (only joking!)
Sharon X = Sharon the Tenth (joking again!)

Did you know?
When Prince Charles is King, he will be Charles III (the Third). When Prince William is King, he will be William V (the Fifth).

Contents

Wales against the world

1 Write ENGLAND and WALES in the correct places on the map.

2 Complete the sentences.

1   The capital of England is   L __ N __ O __

2   The capital of Wales is   C __ R __ I __ F __

(You don't know? Read the text and find out!)

3 Read about the Welsh flag* and colour it.

Scotland

• Edinburgh

GREAT BRITAIN

There is a red dragon in the centre of the Welsh flag. Colour the dragon red. The top of the flag is white. Leave the top white. The bottom of the flag is dark green. Colour the bottom dark green.

Wales

Never call a Welsh person 'English'. They don't like it! The Welsh are special people with a special history. They are Celts. The first Celts – people from Europe – came to live in Wales in 700 BC. (BC = before Christ*).

Then, the Romans lived in Britain and Wales. After that, 'Angle' and 'Saxon' people came from Europe to England but Wales stayed an independent* country for about 800 years.

In 1282, the Welsh prince died in a fight with English soldiers. King Edward I of England captured* Wales. He called his young son the 'Prince of Wales'. Today, the Prince of Wales is Prince Charles, the son of Queen Elizabeth II. Charles's first wife, Diana, was the Princess of Wales; his second wife, Camilla, is not.

In 1485, a Welshman, Henry Tudor, became King of England. He was Henry VII. His son – Henry VIII – made Wales a part of England in 1536. After that, London ruled* Wales. Everyone used the English language for important things. Young people started

to forget the Welsh language. Some Welsh people were not happy about this.

In 1997, Wales got a Welsh Assembly – a place for Welsh people to talk about Welsh problems. It's in the capital, Cardiff. Today, children in Wales learn Welsh at school. Thousands of people speak Welsh. There is Welsh language TV too. *Cymru* means *Wales* in Welsh!

CYMRU

4 Who are these people? Write the words in the sentences.

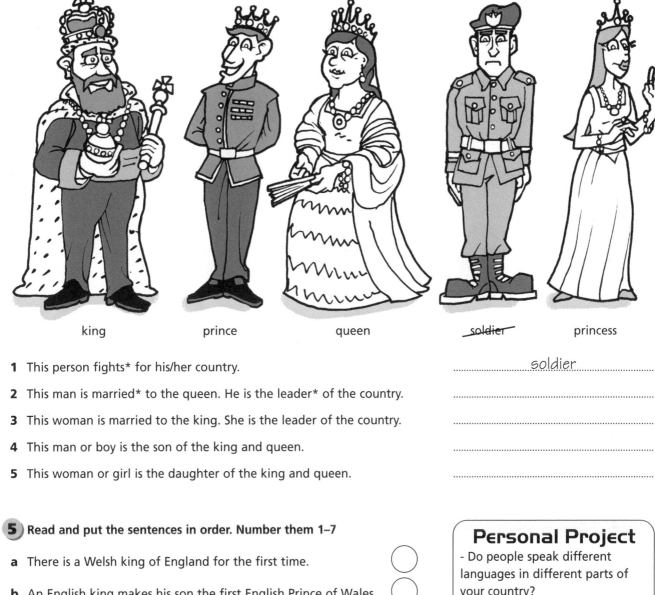

king   prince   queen   ~~soldier~~   princess

1 This person fights* for his/her country.   *soldier*

2 This man is married* to the queen. He is the leader* of the country.

3 This woman is married to the king. She is the leader of the country.

4 This man or boy is the son of the king and queen.

5 This woman or girl is the daughter of the king and queen.

5 Read and put the sentences in order. Number them 1–7

a There is a Welsh king of England for the first time.   ◯

b An English king makes his son the first English Prince of Wales.   ◯

c The Anglo Saxons arrive in England.   ◯

d The Celts come to live in Wales.   ①

e The Romans arrive in Wales.   ◯

f Wales gets an Assembly.   ◯

g Henry VIII makes Wales part of England.   ◯

Personal Project
- Do people speak different languages in different parts of your country?
- Choose one part of your country and find out more about its history.

* What is it in your language? Find out!

6 Put the ordered sentences in activity 5 into a past tense paragraph. Use *first, then, next, after that, in the end.*

Scotland for ever!

1 Write north, south, east and west on the compass. Draw Hadrian's wall.

A long, high wall – Hadrian's wall – divides England and Scotland. In Roman times this wall stopped the 'Picts' in the north from entering Roman Britain in the south. (The Picts were the early people of Scotland.) You can visit Hadrian's wall today. It goes between Bowness in the west and Wallsend in the east.

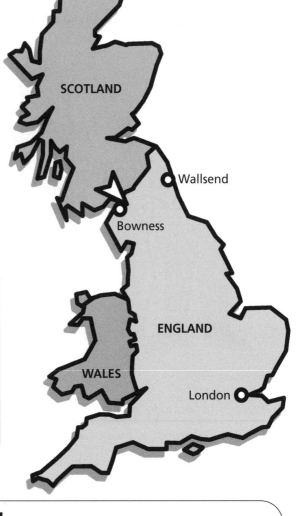

SCOTLAND

Wallsend

Bowness

ENGLAND

WALES

London

Scotland

For many years, Scotland was an independent* country. But in 1286 the Scottish king died without a son. England's King Edward I became the leader of Scotland. The Scots were not happy with this. The Scottish fighter William Wallace fought against the English. He was very brave*. (People called him 'Braveheart'.) But he lost. Edward took Wallace to London and executed* him.

The Scots didn't stop fighting. In 1314 Robert Bruce fought the English and won. He became King Robert I of Scotland.

A lot of Scots preferred France to England. King James V of Scotland married a French princess. After he died, his daughter, Mary, became Queen of Scots. She was very young.

Mary married three times. Her first husband was the French King, but he died a year later. Her second husband was her cousin*, Lord Darnley. They had a son, James. Then Darnley died. Mary quickly married again. She married her husband's killer, people said. Mary was in trouble! She asked her English cousin,

Queen Elizabeth I, for help. That was a mistake. Elizabeth executed* Mary to stop her from becoming Queen of England.

Elizabeth died in 1603 with no children. Now Mary's son, James, was King of Scotland and England. In 1707, Scotland became a part of England and lost its Parliament*. In 1997, Scotland got its own Parliament again.

2 Read and complete these sentences in Hadrian's wall with the correct words.

1 Hadrian's wall is in the _ ☐ _ _ _ of England.

2 The wall goes from Bowness to _ _ _ _ _ _ ☐

3 Robert Bruce fought against the ☐ _ _ _ _ _ _ .

4 'Braveheart's' real name was _ _ _ _ _ _ _ ☐ _ _ _ _ _ _ .

5 A lot of Scottish people liked _ _ _ _ _ ☐ more than England.

6 The Queen of England's name was _ _ _ _ _ _ _ ☐ _ _ .

7 Mary's son became ☐ _ _ _ of Scotland and England.

3 How old was Mary when she became Queen? Write the boxed letters to find her age.

_O_ _ _ _ _ _ _ _

4 Read the puzzle and find the answers.

A small animal finally built her home after trying many times. Robert Bruce learnt from her. He fought the English one last time, and won.

t h e s c a p i t a l p o f i s c o t l a n d d i s e e d i n b u r g h r

1 Find the fact about Scotland in Bruce's sword and write it. Careful with capital letters!

Fact: ....

2 Write the extra letters to find the animal. (It's on this page!)

Animal: _ _ _ _ _ _ _

5 Correct Mike Mistake's History exam answers. Put *dis-*, *im-*, *in-* or *un-* in front of the underlined words.

1 Edward I .dis̲liked William Wallace.

2 Queen Elizabeth I was ....married when she died.

3 Mary, Queen of Scots was ....lucky in her choice of husbands.

4 Hadrian's wall made it ....possible for the Picts to enter Roman Britain.

5 James V of Scotland was ....friendly towards the English.

6 It is ....correct to call people from Scotland 'Scotch'.

Personal Project

- Which people fought in the past for your country, or your part of the country, to be free?
- Choose one of them and find out more about his or her life.

* What is it in your language? Find out!

The Irish question

1 **What do you know about Ireland? Do the Ireland quiz.**

NORTHERN IRELAND

IRISH REPUBLIC

Ireland quiz

1 **Which saint* is the patron* of Ireland? When is his day?**
  a Saint Andrew – Saint Andrew's day is 20th November.
  b Saint Patrick – Saint Patrick's day is 17th March.

2 **When was the Great Irish Potato Famine*?**
  a in the 1840s
  b in the 1940s

3 **What Christian Church do most people follow in the North of Ireland?**
  a the Protestant Church
  b the Roman Catholic Church

4 **What Christian Church do most people follow in the South of Ireland?**
  a the Protestant Church
  b the Roman Catholic Church

5 **What is 'Sinn Fein'?**
  a an Irish terrorist group
  b an Irish political party

6 **What is 'the IRA'?**
  a an Irish terrorist group
  b an Irish political party

Check your answers quickly in the text.

Ireland

The Celts came to Ireland in 300 BC. They made pots and farmed the land. From 400 AD <u>Christians</u> like Saint Patrick arrived. Saint Patrick became a very special person to the Irish. He is the patron saint of Ireland.

In 1607 many important Irish lords* in the north of Ireland left the country. James I gave their lands to Englishmen and Scotsmen. They were Protestant Christians. But Ireland was a Catholic Christian country. Soon Irish Protestants had the best jobs, good land, and money. Catholics had the worst jobs, poor land, and no money.

In 1800 Ireland became part of Great Britain. Then in the 1840s the potatoes in Irish farms went bad. There was a famine*. Many poor Irish people got hungry and died. A lot emigrated* to America or England, looking for a better life.

Many people in Ireland – mainly in the south – wanted to be independent. In 1918 the Irish political party Sinn Fein formed a parliament* in Dublin. The IRA (Irish Republican <u>Army</u>) protected it. In 1921 Northern Ireland chose to stay part of Britain. In 1948 the South became an <u>independent</u> country – The Irish <u>Republic</u>. The problem was, there were still some Catholics in the North.

From the 1970s the IRA attacked ordinary people with guns and bombs*. Many people died or were hurt in these <u>terrorist</u> attacks. The Protestants in the North fought back. Today, the terrorist attacks have stopped, but the problem hasn't gone away. The IRA wants Northern Ireland to join the Catholic Irish Republic. Protestant groups in the North want Northern Ireland to stay part of Britain. Most ordinary Irish people just want peace*.

What's for dinner, Mum?

Potato soup - without the potatoes!

2 Match the meanings with the underlined words in the text.

1 a group of people fighting on one side   ....army....................................

2 a country with a president, not a king   ....

3 someone who kills or hurts people to achieve a goal   ....

4 religious people who follow Christ   ....

5 separate and free   ....

3 Read the text again and put the sentences in order.

a Ireland became part of Great Britain.   *A*

b The IRA attacked people with bombs.   *L*

c The Irish Republic began.   *S*

d St Patrick came to Ireland.   *M*

e James I gave land to English and Scots people.   *R*

f The Celts came to Ireland.   *E* 1

g Britain hoped for an end to the terrorist attacks.   *E*

h Sinn Fein formed an Irish parliament in Dublin.   *D*

i Important lords in the North of Ireland left the country.   *E*

j Many Irish people left for America.   *L*

k Northern Ireland stayed with Britain and the South became a Free State.   *I*

4 Ireland is a very green island. Put the letters in the potatoes in order to find a romantic name for it:

THE E _ _ _ _ _ _ _   _ _ _ _

5 Complete the 'Irish shamrock' leaves with the missing parts of the verbs.

come
came   come
1

get
2

be
3

leave
4
give
5

go
6

become
7

choose
8

Personal Project

- Which terrorist groups do you know about? What have they done to get in the news? What are they fighting for, or against?
- Choose one group and find out more about it.

* What is it in your language? Find out!

Crazy* kings

1 King Henry VIII had six wives. Do you know their names? Read the text to find out.

Henry VIII (1491-1547, King from 1509)

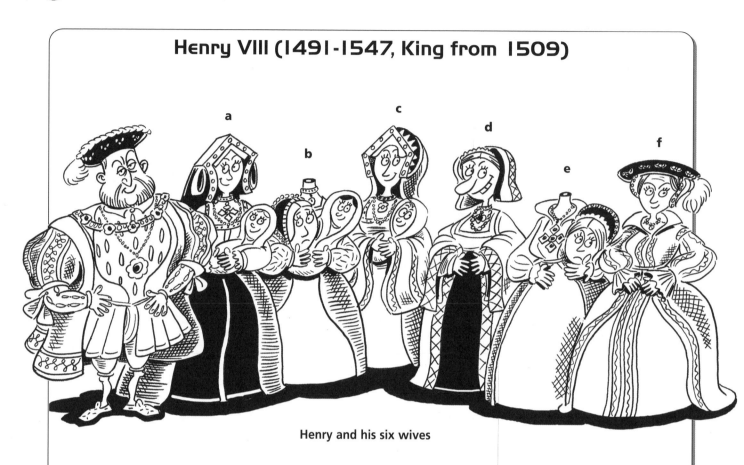

Henry and his six wives

When Henry VIII became king he was 18. He danced and sang well. Everyone loved him. But he needed a son. His first wife - Catherine of Aragon - was Spanish. Catherine and Henry had a daughter, Mary. Henry wasn't happy. He wanted a divorce*. The Church* in Rome said 'no'. So Henry started the Church of England. Then he and Catherine divorced.

Henry then married Anne Boleyn. She had a daughter, Elizabeth. But Anne was in love with her brother, and Henry heard about it. He sent her to the Tower of London. There they cut off her head, or 'beheaded'

her. Next Henry married Jane Seymour. She had a son, Edward, but then she died.

After that Henry married a German princess, Anne of Cleves. She was ugly. 'She looks like a horse,' Henry said. They soon divorced. Then Henry married Catherine Howard. She was 20 and beautiful, and Henry was 49. Catherine lost her head when Henry heard about her boyfriend. Henry's last wife was Katherine Parr. She was nice to Henry - and she survived* him! Henry's son Edward was the next king.

2 What happened to Henry's wives? Write these words next to the names. They make a rhyme that English children learn at school.

survived	died	beheaded
beheaded	divorced	divorced

1 Catherine of Aragon ....

2 Anne Boleyn ....

3 Jane Seymour ....

4 Anne of Cleves ....

5 Catherine Howard ....

6 Katherine Parr ....

3 George III was a crazy king. What do you think he did? Read the text and find out.

a He talked to trees.
b He lost America.
c He gave Buckingham Palace* to his wife.
d He hated his son.

George III (1738-1820, King from 1760)

George III had 15 children. He loved his wife, Charlotte. (He gave Buckingham Palace to her!) He studied the stars and he loved reading. He liked country life too. He knew all about animals, fruit and vegetables. The British liked him and called him 'The Farmer King'. But Britain lost America under George III!

In later life George III went crazy. He talked to trees and shouted 'peacock*' all the time. He couldn't rule* the country. His oldest son - George, Prince of Wales - ruled it for him. George III hated the Prince. When George III died, the Prince became King George IV.

4 These sentences compare Henry VIII and George III. Read both texts again and tick the correct column (H for Henry or G for George).

	H		G
1 He was younger when he became king.	✓	t	○
2 He was older when he died.	○	h	○
3 He had more children.	○	a	○
4 He was king for longer.	○	n	○
5 He had lots of wives.	○	u	○
6 He had a terrible son.	○	o	○
7 He started the Church of England.	○	d	○
8 He liked reading.	○	v	○
9 He knew about fruit and vegetables.	○	e	○
10 He liked dancing and singing.	○	o	○
11 His son Edward was king after him.	○	r	○
12 He studied the stars.	○	r	○

5 Write the letters in the stars to find the name of each king's family.

1 Henry VIII's family name was T _ _ _ _

2 George III's family name was

H _ _ _ _ _ _

Personal Project

- Were there any crazy rulers in your country? What did they do?
- Choose one of them and find out more about him or her.

* What is it in your language? Find out!

Cool queens

1 **Look at these two famous queens. Which queen …**
  1 … lived in the 1500s?
  2 … lived in the 1800s?
  3 … said 'We are not amused*!'?
  4 … said 'I am married to England!'?

What do you think? Read the texts to check your ideas.

Elizabeth I (born 1533, Queen from 1558 to 1603)

Elizabeth's sister, Mary, was the Queen of England from 1553 to 1558. Elizabeth liked the Church of England, but Mary hated it. So she locked Elizabeth in the Tower of London. When Mary died, Elizabeth became queen. She spoke five languages, was tall and thin, and had fair skin and red hair. The Spanish King and a French Prince wanted to marry her when she was young. But she said 'no' to them. She said, 'I am married to England.' She painted her face white, wore a red <u>wig</u>, and became 'The Virgin* Queen'.

Painters had <u>to paint</u> Elizabeth as a beautiful young woman even when she was old. But she was a popular queen. Elizabethan England was famous for writers like Shakespeare, and for sailors like Francis Drake, and Walter Raleigh. English people in America gave the name 'Virginia' to their new home. The name came from Elizabeth, the Virgin queen.

Victoria (born 1818, Queen from 1837 to 1901)

Queen Victoria was queen of <u>the United Kingdom</u> for 64 years - the longest time on the <u>throne</u> of any British King or Queen. She married her German <u>cousin</u>, Prince Albert. He worked hard to help her. (He also brought the idea of Christmas trees to Britain from Germany!) Victoria loved Albert, and they had nine children. When Albert died in 1861, Victoria wore black clothes for the rest of her life.

Victoria was very popular with the British. In 1887 there were big street parties for her. Signs everywhere said, '50 Years Our Queen'. In 1897 there were more parties for her after 60 years as queen. Victoria was a small woman - only 5 feet (1.5 metres) tall. And when she was old she got very fat. But she was a great queen. In the Victorian age Britain had a large Empire* – with lands in Africa, India, Hong Kong, Australia, New Zealand and Canada.

2 **Match the underlined words in the texts with their meanings.**

1 to put colour on

...................to paint...................

2 the son (or daughter) of your father's (or mother's) brother (or sister)

....

3 false hair

....

4 a king or queen sits on this special chair

....

5 England, Wales, Scotland and Ireland together as one country

....

3 **Read the texts again. Mark these sentences E (Elizabeth) or V (Victoria).**

	E	V
1 She was queen for 45 years.	✓ R	○ T
2 The Spanish king wanted to marry her.	○ O	○ H
3 She wore black for many years.	○ O	○ B
4 She had red hair and a white face.	○ E	○ M
5 She married her cousin.	○ A	○ R
6 She had nine children.	○ S	○ T
7 She wore a wig when she was older.	○ D	○ B
8 She spoke five languages.	○ U	○ R
9 Her husband brought Christmas trees to England.	○ I	○ D
10 She was a short and fat old woman.	○ G	○ L
11 A French prince wanted to marry her.	○ E	○ H
12 She had a large Empire.	○ T	○ Y

4 **The love of Queen Elizabeth I's life was a married man. Look at the boxes you ticked in activity 3. Write the letters to find his name.**

R _ _ _ _ _   _ _ _ _ _ _

5 **Write the superlative of the adjectives in the Christmas trees.**

★1 ....the........... ....fairest........... fair

★2 .... popular

★3 .... large

★4 .... thin

★5 .... great

★6 .... white

★7 .... fat

★8 .... famous

★9 .... red

★10 .... big

Personal Project
- Were there any cool queens in your country? What did they do?
- Choose one queen and find out more about her.

* What is it in your language? Find out!

Romantic royals

1 **Match the words with their meanings.**

> assassinate   captain   div<u>i</u>orce
> governo<u>r</u>   <u>n</u>avy   r<u>o</u>yal   ~~weird~~

1 very strange ....*weird*............

2 the most important person on a
ship; an army officer ....

3 a group of people that fight in
ships on the sea for their country ....

4 to stop being married ....

5 to kill someone for political reasons ....

6 belonging to a king's or
queen's family ....

7 someone that makes the laws in a
country that belongs to an empire ....

2 **What is the family name of today's British royals?
Put the underlined letters in activity 1 in order to
find it.**

W _ _ _ _ _ _

3 **Look at the photos. What do you know about
Edward VIII and Prince Charles? Mark these
sentences E (Edward) or C (Charles).**

1 He was born in the 1890s.

2 He was born in the 1940s.

3 He used to talk to plants.

4 He left the throne of England for love.

5 He married an American.

6 He has two sons - William and Harry.

What do you think? Read the texts to check your ideas.

Edward VIII and Wallace Simpson

Edward VIII was the son of King George
V. He was born in 1894. Like all the oldest
sons of British Kings, he became Prince of
Wales. He was handsome and popular
with the British people, and he loved
parties. When King George V died in
1936, Edward became king.

Edward wanted to marry an American,
Wallace Simpson. She had divorced
twice and the Archbishop* of Canterbury
said that the King (as the leader of the
Church of England) could not marry a
divorced woman.

After 11 months Edward gave up the
throne of England for the woman that
he loved. He became the Duke* of
Windsor. He married Wallace and spent
the rest of his life abroad. He was the
governor of the Bahamas for a time.
Some people say that the Duke was
friendly with the German leader, Adolf
Hitler, because he hoped to go back to
England as king if the Germans won
the Second World War.

Charles, Diana – and Camilla!

Prince Charles was born in Buckingham Palace in 1948. He had some weird habits when he was younger – like talking to plants. After school he studied at Cambridge University. Later he joined the Navy, and was the captain of a ship. In 1981 he married Lady Diana Spencer. They had two sons, William (born 1982) and Harry (born 1984). But Diana became unhappy when she learnt that Charles had a married lover, Camilla Parker-Bowles.

Charles had first met Camilla in 1970. He fell in love with her at once. But she was older than him, and she had had boyfriends before.

Camilla divorced her husband in 1995. In 1996 Charles and Diana divorced. The next year Diana died in a car crash in Paris. Some people think that she was assassinated. In 2005 Charles finally married the love of his life, Camilla Parker-Bowles.

4 Read the texts again. Join the sentences correctly.

1 1936 was the year…

2 The Archbishop of Canterbury was the person…

3 Wallace Simpson was the woman…

4 The Duke of Windsor was the title…

5 Adolf Hitler was the German leader…

6 Cambridge was the university…

7 1970 was the year…

8 1981 was the year…

9 1997 was the year…

10 2005 was the year…

a that Edward married.

b that Charles met Camilla.

c that Edward VIII was king for 11 months.

d that the Duke was friendly with.

e that Edward was given after he left the throne.

f that said Edward couldn't marry a divorced woman.

g that Prince Charles studied at.

h that Princess Diana died.

i that Charles married Camilla.

j that Charles married Lady Diana Spencer.

5 What do we call it when a king gives up the throne because he doesn't want to rule anymore? Put the letters in the hearts in order to find the word.

A _ _ _ _ _ _ _ _

* What is it in your language? Find out!

Personal Project

- Were there any famous royal couples in your country's history? What happened to them?
- Choose one royal couple and find out more about them.

The Queen's Homes

The Queen* of England (Elizabeth II) has got lots of homes. Sometimes she lives at Buckingham Palace* in London and sometimes at Windsor Castle* in Windsor. (She also has a home - Balmoral Castle - in Scotland!)

1 Write the verbs in the gaps.

> lived   had   stays   ~~built~~   started

Buckingham Palace

In 1705, the Duke* of Buckingham **1** .... *built* .... Buckingham Palace. Queen Victoria **2** .... there in 1837. After that, different kings* and queens lived in the palace. Today, Queen Elizabeth II often **3** .... there. When she is at 'home', a flag* flies from the roof*.

Windsor Castle

William I (William the First) **4** .... to build* this castle in the 1070s. The castle is a favourite place for royal weddings*. Prince Charles and Camilla Parker-Bowles **5** .... a big party in the castle after their wedding in 2005.

2 Match the pictures on the next page with the numbered texts.

1 Money problems ....
The Queen opened Buckingham Palace to the public* for the first time in 1993. Why? Because she needed money after a big fire at Windsor Castle. The fire lasted for 15 hours and it destroyed* a lot of rooms.

2 Big Houses ....
Buckingham Palace has more than 500 rooms and 78 bathrooms. 19 of the rooms are open to the public for two months each year. Windsor Castle is a lot bigger – it has over 1,000 rooms!

3 The Royal* Guard* ....
Every day, lots of tourists* stand in front of the palace to watch the Changing of the Guard. The Guards wear red jackets and 'bearskins' (very big black hats). They mustn't smile at the tourists when they are working. This is sometimes very difficult!

4 The gardens ....
The gardens at Buckingham Palace are very big. In 2002, the Queen had a big pop concert* there to celebrate* 50 years of being Queen. She also has big tea parties there and invites different people to them. For a picnic*, go to Windsor. The gardens there are bigger and they are always open.

5 Not invited ....
In 1982 the Queen woke up at Buckingham Palace with a surprise. There was a strange* man sitting on her bed! His name was Michael Fagan. They talked for half an hour. Fagan asked the queen for a cigarette*, but she couldn't give him one. She doesn't smoke. There are 200 bedrooms in the Palace. How did he find the right one?

A

B

C

D

E

3 Complete these sentences with words from the text. The first letters make the name of the Queen's favourite kind of dog.

1 Windsor <u>C a s t l e</u> is older than Buckingham Palace.

2 Only 19 of the rooms at Buckingham Palace are _ _ _ _ to the public.

3 The British _ _ _ _ _ Family have a lot of houses.

4 The _ _ _ _ _ _ _ at Buckingham Palace have beautiful trees and flowers.

5 The Queen sometimes _ _ _ _ _ _ _ _ people to parties at the palace.

The dog is a <u>C</u>.....................

4 Find seven mistakes in the e-mail from Mike Mistake.

To: jess@email.com
Cc:
Subject: Hi from London!
Account:

Hi Jess
Yesterday we went to Windsor Castle and today we went to Buckingham Palace. I'm so tired! They are just two of Queen Victoria's *Elizabeth's* houses! There were a lot of people at Windsor. It's a castle and William the First started to build it in the 1170s so it's very old. There was a fire there in 1982, but now it's fine. The gardens are small so we went for a walk and we had a picnic. That was great. Buckingham Palace was a bit boring. It has about a hundred rooms and we saw nineteen of them. They're all the same! After that, we saw the Changing of the Guard. They wear blue uniforms and funny hats. The Queen sometimes invites people for coffee at the palace, but she didn't invite me! Maybe next time!
Mike

Personal Project

- Where did the rulers of your country live in the past? Did they have different houses?
- Choose one of their houses and find out more about it.

* What is it in your language? Find out!

A prison and a palace

1 **Match the words with the pictures.**

bridge clock crown execute maze moon prison raven tennis tower

1 ....tower............

2 ....

3 ....

4 ....

5 ....

6 ....

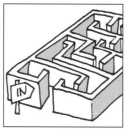

7 ....

8 ....

9 ....

10 ....

2 **Complete the text about The Towert of London with words from Exercise 1.**

The Tower of London

Hello. I'm a guard at the Tower of London. People call us 'beefeaters'. Perhaps it's because in the past they paid us with meat, not money.

The Tower is over 900 years old and it's next to the River Thames and Tower **1** ....Bridge.... . William I built it as a castle, then it was a zoo*, but it is most famous as a **2** .... Many kings and queens stayed here. They **3** ....d some of them. The Tower of London isn't just one **4** .... There are lots of towers, some big and some small. One is called the Bloody* Tower because two young princes died there in 1483.

The Crown Jewels* are at the Tower. Many kings and queens wore these beautiful **5** ....s and jewels.

Big, black birds called **6** ....s guard the Tower with me. Without ravens at the Tower, people say it's the end of the kings and queens of England. So be careful with our birds!

Hampton Court

Hi there. I'm a guide at Hampton Court Palace on the north bank of the River Thames. Hampton Court was the favourite home of King Henry VIII. He lived in 'Tudor' times and I'm wearing Tudor clothes. Cardinal* Wolsey built Hampton Court, but Henry took it from him in 1529. Henry loved his home at Hampton Court. He looked after* it very well too.

3 Find out more about Hampton Court. Do the maze to answer these questions.

1 What was one of Henry's favourite sports? Was it tennis or football? ....*tennis*.......

2 What does the astronomical* clock tell you? Is it the size of the moon or the size or the sun? ....

3 What did Henry put in the garden in 1769? (It's still there today!) Is it a vine or an apple tree? ....

4 Which animals can you see in the parks around the palace? Is it deer or sheep? ....

5 What happened in 1986? Was there a fire or a flood? ....

[A maze puzzle with icons across the top: tennis racket and ball, football, another ball, astronomical clock, grapes/vine, apple tree, deer, sheep, fire, flood. Numbered exits 1, 2, 3, 4, 5 at the bottom.]

4 Make sentences. Follow the example. Then write TOL (The Tower of London) or HC (Hampton Court).

Which building?

1 William I / build / it   ....*William I built it.*.......   ....*TOL*.......

2 Henry VIII / live / there   ....

3 the guides / be / in Tudor clothes   ....

4 Beefeaters / get / meat as pay   ....

5 they / execute / a lot of people there   ....

6 two young princes / die / there   ....

5 Find the words.

1 The R i v e r T h a m e s is near the Tower and Hampton Court.

2 You can see the ☐_ _ _ _ _ _ _ _ _ _ at the Tower.

3 Hampton Court was the ☐_ _ ○ of Henry VIII.

4 The Tower is hundreds of years _ _ ○

5 _☐☐☐_ _ _ _ ○_ _ _ _ _ built Hampton Court.

6 Beefeaters are _ _ ○○○_ at the Tower of London.

6 Find the names of the Princes in the Tower. Use the letters in the squares and circles.

○ _ _ _ _ _ _ _ and

☐ _ _ _ _ _ _ _

Personal Project
- Are there any old prisons or palaces in your country? Which famous people lived in them?
- Find out more about one prison or palace.

* What is it in your language? Find out!

Top universities: Oxford and Cambridge

**Oxford and Cambridge are the top two universities in England.
Some people call the two unversities together 'Oxbridge'!**

1 True or False? What do you think?

1 Cambridge University is older than Oxford University. ....
2 Oxford has more colleges than Cambridge. ....
3 The first Oxford students studied in Paris. ....
4 Teachers at Oxford and Cambridge before the 19th century couldn't marry. ....
5 No women studied at the universities until the 20th century. ....
6 Every year, the two universities compete in a swimming race. ....

Read the guidebook and check your ideas.

2 Match the titles with the numbered parts of the text.

> The first students   No married teachers   An exciting competition
> Women students   Staying at the universities   ~~Ancient universities~~

1 .... Ancient Universities ....

The towns of Oxford and Cambridge have some of the finest buildings in Britain. They are famous for their universities, the oldest in England. All the students live and study in a college. Cambridge has 31 colleges and Oxford has 39. Oxford's first college started in 1249. Cambridge's first college opened in 1281.

2 ....

Before the 12th century, people who wanted a good education went to the Sorbonne in Paris. Then, in 1167, all English students in Paris moved to Oxford. Some people say King Henry II told them to move. Others say the French threw them out! The students went to study in Oxford monasteries* and that was the beginning of Oxford University.

3 ....

The Church was very important in Oxford and Cambridge for many years. For example, until the 19th century the university teachers were almost like priests* and they couldn't marry.

4 ....

Women started studying later than men. The first women's college at Cambridge opened in 1869 and at Oxford in 1878. Today, three Cambridge colleges and one Oxford college are for women only. Men and women study together in the others.

5 ....

Every year the universities compete in a rowing* race over 7 kilometres of the Thames. Each boat has eight male rowers and a cox*, who must be a very light man or woman. The first race was in 1829 and it became a yearly race in 1839. All the students really want their university to win!

6 ....

People can stay in rooms at Oxford and Cambridge when the students are on holiday. Some rooms are modern but the older rooms are more interesting (and more uncomfortable!). They often have low ceilings*, small windows and a view of the square or 'quadrangle' in the middle of the college. Imagine sleeping in the same room as an ex Prime Minister* or eating at the same table as Lawrence of Arabia!

Students past and present

3 Which rules is this student breaking?

February 6th 1568

Rules for students

~ *Students are not allowed to wear boots in public*
~ *Curly hair is not allowed. Penalty*: 6 shillings*.*
~ *Students must not go near shops that sell wine* or tobacco*.*
~ *Students must be back in their college before 9 in the evening.*
~ *Students must not carry dangerous weapons* (only bows and arrows when they are using them for fun.)*

4 Label the clothes.

1 ....
2 ....
3 ....
4 ....
5 ....

February 6th 2005
RULES
Students must buy the following clothes:
Men
1 gown, 1 cap, 1 bow-tie (white)
Women
1 gown, 1 cap, 1 black ribbon
Students will wear these clothes on special days, for example: on Day 1 of university.
Bicycles
It is not necessary to buy one of these, but they are very useful for travelling round the city and between colleges.

5 Oxford and Cambridge have had some very famous graduates. Can you match the people with their activities?

Oxford

1 Sir Thomas More

2 Oscar Wilde

3 Hugh Grant

4 Margaret Thatcher

5 Rowan Atkinson

a Prime Minister of Britain in the 80s and 90s

b film star

c comic film and TV star (Mr Bean)

d writer

e politician at the time of Henry VIII

Cambridge

1 Charles Darwin

2 Isaac Newton

3 Winston Churchill

4 Lord Byron

5 Stephen Hawking

a Romantic poet*

b Prime Minister of Britain in the 40s and 50s

c Theory* of Evolution* scientist

d scientist who wrote *A Brief* History of Time*

e mathematician* who 'discovered' gravity*

Personal Project
- Are there any old universities in your country? Which famous people studied at them?
- Choose one of these univerities and find out more about it.

* What is it in your language? Find out!

Sea explorers

No one lives very far from the sea in Britain so the sea is very important in British history. Many years ago, the only way to see the world was by boat. Some sailors* did exciting things.

Sir Francis Drake (1542-1596)

1 Match the pictures with the different parts of the text about Drake.

1 b   2   3   4

a

b

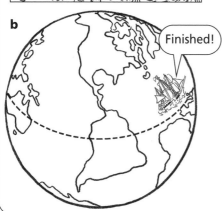

Finished!

1 Drake was a sailor at the time of Queen* Elizabeth I. He sailed* around the world (1577-1580). He was the first English person to do this.

2 Drake sailed to South America and took money and other things back to England. The Queen was very happy with the money because England had money problems at this time. She went onto Drake's boat, the *Golden* Hind**, and said, 'Now you are Sir Francis Drake.' (Only important people have 'Sir' before their first name.)

3 In 1588, there was a war* between the English navy* and the Spanish navy (the Armada). The Spanish weren't lucky. They lost many boats because the weather in the North Sea was terrible. This helped the English and they won* the war. The Queen was happy with Drake again.

4 Drake died in 1596 in the West Indies. Before he died, he asked to see his favourite drum. There are many stories about the drum. Today, it is in Drake's house in England. Before a war, people say you can hear the sound of a drum – Drake's drum!

c

d

GOLDEN HIND

2 Read the text again and match the sentence halves.

1 Drake was the first English sailor
2 The Queen needed money
3 The Queen liked Drake
4 The name of Drake's boat
5 When Drake had money
6 In the war against Spain
7 Drake died
8 Drake's drum is

a and she called him 'Sir'.   C
b in the West Indies.   T
c the bad weather helped England.   U
d in his house in England.   S
e was the *Golden Hind*.   O
f because England had problems.   O
g to go around the world.   C
h he bought a house.   N

3 Put the letters in the drums in the correct order to find out which fruit Drake found.   c _ _ _ _ _ _ _

4 Match the titles with the different parts of the text about Raleigh.

a An Irish house   **b** Exploring America   **c** ~~The Queen's favourite~~   **d** A sad end   **e** Cloak and puddle*

Sir Walter Raleigh (1554 – 1618)

1 .... *c The Queen's favourite*

Queen Elizabeth I liked Walter Raleigh more than Francis Drake! (He is also a 'Sir', as you can see.) He won wars for her in Ireland and France.

2 ....

There is a famous story about Raleigh: One day, the Queen went for a walk in the street. Suddenly, she saw a dirty puddle in front of her. Raleigh quickly put his cloak on the puddle, and the Queen walked over it. She didn't get her shoes wet or dirty! From that day, Raleigh was the Queen's favourite man!

3 ....

Raleigh was an explorer. He sailed to different countries. He went to North America and he tried to start an English town there. He left some English men and women in America. When the boats went back with food a few months later, the people weren't there. What happened to them? We don't know.

4 ....

Raleigh was a good spy*. Some people wanted to kill Queen Elizabeth. They wanted Mary (the Queen of Scotland) to be Queen of England. Raleigh learnt about this plan and he told Elizabeth. She gave him a big house and gardens in Ireland to say 'thank you'.

5 ....

But after Elizabeth died in 1603, Raleigh wasn't so lucky. The new king, James I, put him in prison* in London. Raleigh came out of prison in 1612. He went to South America looking for El Dorado, a fantastic city full of gold*. He didn't find it, and there were problems. Raleigh killed some people, and he did not bring any money back to England for the king. The king executed* Raleigh in 1618.

5 Raleigh brought two new things back to Britain.
What were they? Look at the picture clues and unscramble the letters.

1 OTACBOC

_ _ _ _ _ _ _

2 TOPATOSE

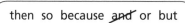

_ _ _ _ _ _ _

6 Complete the text about Drake and Raleigh with these words.

Drake and Raleigh were explorers **1** ....*and*........ they worked for Queen

Elizabeth I. They sometimes killed people in wars **2** .... the Queen

liked them. They gave her money **3** .... she called them 'Sir'. The

Queen needed more money at this time **4** .... England had money

problems. **5** .... Queen Elizabeth died, and James I was king.

Everything changed after that.

Were Drake and Raleigh good men **6** .... bad men?

What do you think?

then so because ~~and~~ or but

Personal Project

- Did your country have any famous sea explorers in the past? Where did they go? What did they do?
- Find out more about one of them.

* What is it in your language?
Find out!

Extreme explorers

'Extreme' explorers go to the hottest, coldest, highest, and most dangerous places on earth.

Extreme cold

Extreme heat

1 Imagine you are in the Antarctic, travelling to the South Pole. What's it like? Choose the correct words.

1 The weather is (freezing)/ boiling.

2 There's a lot of sand / snow and ice.

3 There are penguins and seals / camels and crocodiles.

4 You're wearing fur / cotton clothes.

5 You're travelling by sledge / camel train.

6 Dogs / Camels pull your transport*.

7 Your fingers are black. Perhaps you've got frostbite* / a cold!

You are going to read about two famous British explorers. They both went to the Antarctic.

2 Write the questions in the correct place.
  a How and where did Scott and his men die?
  b ~~Who was Captain Scott?~~
  c Why did things go wrong?
  d What did Scott find when he reached the South Pole?
  e What was Scott's ambition?

Captain Scott (1868-1912)

1 .....Who was Captain Scott?.....
People usually call Captain Robert Falcon Scott 'Scott of the Antarctic'. In 1904, he went further south than any person before him – but he wanted to do more.

2 ....
Scott really wanted to be the first person to reach the South Pole. He didn't do it, but he is still a hero* for many British people.

3 ....
In 1910 Scott tried to reach the South Pole with four other men. They arrived on January 18th 1912. But they weren't the first to reach the Pole. Roald Amundsen from Norway was there three weeks before them. Scott wrote: 'It is a terrible disappointment*.... It will be a difficult return.'

4 ....
In fact, Scott and his men never returned. They all died, hungry and very tired, from frostbite. Scott and the others didn't know it, but they were only 20 kilometres from rescuers when they died.

5 ....
Scott was very brave*. But he made mistakes, and was unlucky with the weather. Amundsen used dogs to pull the sledges, but Scott used men. Also, Scott and his men ate very little, and they ate the wrong food. They became ill with scurvy* because they didn't eat any fruit or vegetables.

3 Read about Shackleton and circle five more extra words. Then put them into the advertisement.

Sir Ernest Shackleton (1874-1922)

Shackleton went (wanted) to the Antarctic with Captain Scott in 1901. After pay Captain Scott's death, Shackleton decided to try to cross the Antarctic by months boat. His boat, the *Endurance**, started out in 1914.

It was another terrible journey. Shackleton's boat went into thick always ice and stayed there. After 281 days the ice moved and broke the ship. The men crossed the ice on foot to Elephant Island. They impossible pulled lifeboats* all the way. Shackleton and five others went 1,000 kilometres across the South Atlantic Ocean to get help. The other 22 men stayed behind.

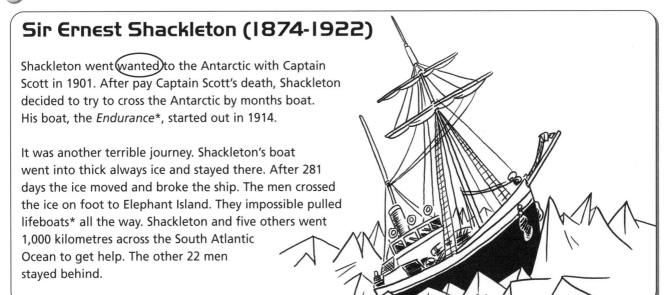

The Times
August 1914

Men **1** wanted for dangerous journey. Poor **2**..................... . Freezing cold. Long **3**..................... of complete darkness*. Danger **4**..................... possible. Death* not **5**..................... . A safe return is not sure. *You will become a hero if you complete the journey.*

4 Look at the complete advertisement. Could you do the job?

5 One of the men on Elephant Island - Frank Wild - wrote to his wife. Snow has fallen on some of the words. Can you complete them?

Elephant Island, 1915

My dear wife,

I hope you are well. It's much ......colder....(1) here than in England. In fact, it's the co............ (2) place in the world! The wor........ (3) times are when it's as black a.......(4) night for 24 hours every day. The be........ (5) times are when we can see well enough to play football.

We sometimes kill a penguin or a seal for food. The seal meat is bet........ (6) than the penguin meat. It isn't .... (7) hard!

Our Captain has gone for help. He's the bra......... (8) man in the world. Take care.
Your loving husband,
Frank

* What is it in your language? Find out!

6 Read and answer the question.

Shackleton and his men landed on the coast* of South Georgia. They walked for 36 hours over mountains to reach a town. Shackleton rescued the men on Elephant Island on August 30th, 1916. All of them were alive, but some of them died soon after. **Do you know why? (The answer is at the bottom of the page.)** Shackleton went to the Antarctic again but he died on his ship in 1922. He is buried* on South Georgia Island.

Personal Project
- Were there any extreme explorers in your country's history? Where did they go? What did they do?
- Find out more about one of them.

ANSWER: They were killed in the First World War.

Explorers in Africa

1 Look at the map of Africa. Write these labels in the correct place:

The River Nile   Lake Victoria   The Sahara desert   east coast   west coast

Until the 19th century, most of Africa was a mystery to the rest of the world. Several European countries had places on the coast for doing business, or 'trading', with the Africans. The rest of Africa was unknown. Anyone who tried to explore inside Africa was killed or became ill and died. But some men (and a few women) wanted adventure. They knew about the dangers but they still wanted to explore Africa!

2 Read the text below and match the dates with the pictures.

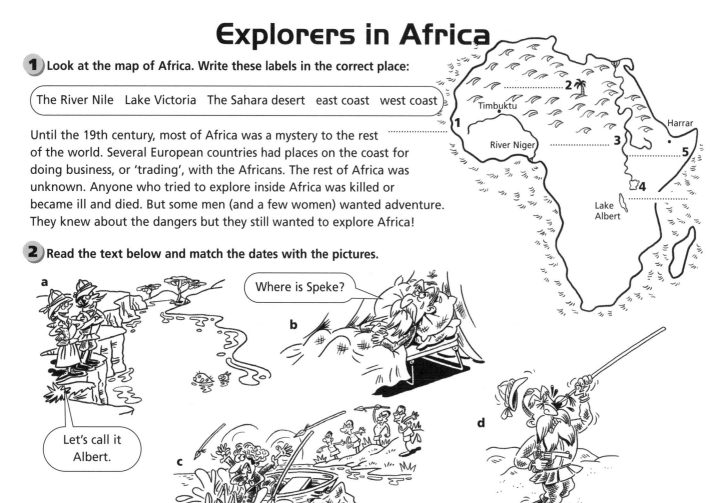

Where is Speke?

Let's call it Albert.

Hot African Explorers' Dates

1796–1805 ....

The Scottish explorer Mungo Park travelled to Timbuktu from the west coast and reached the River Niger. He was the first European to do this. He wrote a book about his adventures. Nine years later, Park returned to the Niger and tried to reach the east coast. His boat hit a rock, and natives attacked Park's men with spears. Park jumped into the river and drowned.

1854 ....

Richard Burton entered the Muslim* city of Harrar in Somalia. He was the first European to leave it alive! He went into the desert for four months, and was hit in the face by a Somali spear. He also wrote a book: *First Footsteps in East Africa.*

1856–1858 ....

Burton went with John Speke to look for the source* of the River Nile. Burton got malaria*. Speke continued without Burton. He found Lake Victoria – but Burton told him where to look! Speke told everyone that he alone had discovered the Nile source. Burton was angry with Speke.

The 1860s ....

Speke and James Grant travelled to the head of Lake Victoria. They were sure they had found the source of the Nile. Then they disappeared. Samuel Baker and his wife, Florence, went to look for them. The Bakers discovered another lake. They called it 'Lake Albert' after Queen Victoria's husband.

3 Who ...

1 ... saw Lake Victoria first?   John Speke   **2** ... was attacked with spears?   ....

3 ... drowned in the river?   ....   **4** ... found Lake Albert?   ....

5 ... left Harrar alive?   ....   **6** ... got angry with Speke?   ....

4 Complete the text about David Livingstone with the past simple of these verbs.

carry   discover   disappear   ~~learn~~
become   shoot   receive   hate

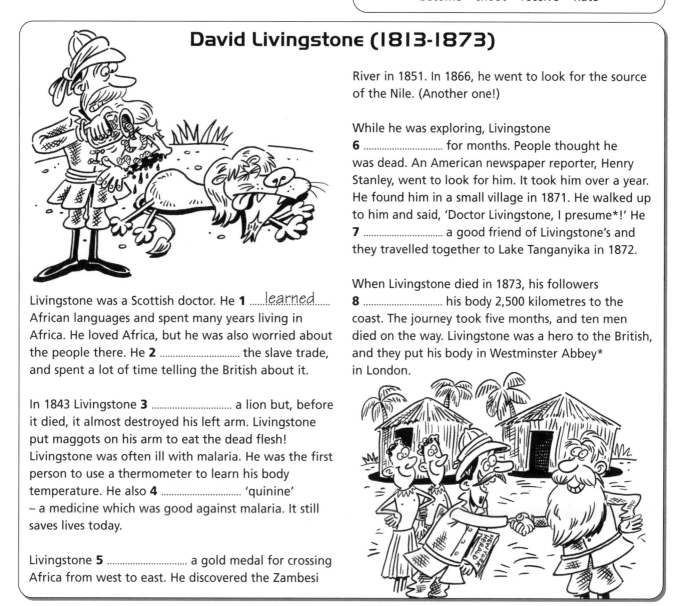

David Livingstone (1813-1873)

Livingstone was a Scottish doctor. He **1** .....learned..... African languages and spent many years living in Africa. He loved Africa, but he was also worried about the people there. He **2** .... the slave trade, and spent a lot of time telling the British about it.

In 1843 Livingstone **3** .... a lion but, before it died, it almost destroyed his left arm. Livingstone put maggots on his arm to eat the dead flesh! Livingstone was often ill with malaria. He was the first person to use a thermometer to learn his body temperature. He also **4** .... 'quinine' – a medicine which was good against malaria. It still saves lives today.

Livingstone **5** .... a gold medal for crossing Africa from west to east. He discovered the Zambesi River in 1851. In 1866, he went to look for the source of the Nile. (Another one!)

While he was exploring, Livingstone **6** .... for months. People thought he was dead. An American newspaper reporter, Henry Stanley, went to look for him. It took him over a year. He found him in a small village in 1871. He walked up to him and said, 'Doctor Livingstone, I presume*!' He **7** .... a good friend of Livingstone's and they travelled together to Lake Tanganyika in 1872.

When Livingstone died in 1873, his followers **8** .... his body 2,500 kilometres to the coast. The journey took five months, and ten men died on the way. Livingstone was a hero to the British, and they put his body in Westminster Abbey* in London.

5 Which words have these meanings?

1 The meat on your body.

f	l	e	s	h

2 A round metal thing that people get when they do something good.

3 A little fat white animal with no legs.

4 To go down under the water and die.

5 A thin glass thing that doctors use to check a patient's temperature.

6 Which part of Livingstone is buried in Africa?
The letters in the shaded boxes tell you.

It's his h _ _ _ _ _

Personal Project
- Did your country have any famous land explorers in the past? Which countries did they visit? What did they do there?
- Find out more about one of them.

* What is it in your language?
Find out!

Florence Nightingale: the lady with the lamp

**In the 19th century in England, rich women did not usually go out to work.
They stayed at home with their families. But some women wanted a
different life. They wanted to learn new things and help people.
Florence Nightingale was one of these women.**

1 Match the questions about Florence Nightingale with the answers.

> **a** Where was she born?   **b** Why is she famous?
> **c** When did she die?   ~~**d** When was she born?~~
> **e** Why do people call her the 'lady with the lamp'?

1 <u>When was she born?</u> .... ?

In 1820.

2 .... ?

In Florence, Italy (but her father and mother were British).

3 .... ?

She was a fantastic nurse*.

4 .... ?

She took a lamp around with her when she was in the hospital.

5 .... ?

In 1910.

2 Complete the text about Florence's life with these words

> food   countries   ~~angry~~   dirty
> student   books   hospital   job

Florence Nightingale

Florence was from a rich family. At first, her mother and father were **1** ....*angry*......... because she wanted to study. They wanted her to marry a rich man. But she read a lot of **2** .... about nursing, and she went to see hospitals in London. In the end her father said, 'You can go to Germany to study nursing, but don't tell anyone!' Florence was a very good **3** .... After Germany, she got an important **4** .... in a London hospital.

In 1854, the Crimean War* began. The wounded* British soldiers* went to a **5** .... in Turkey. Florence went there with 38 nurses. The hospital was very **6** .... The men

never washed. Hundreds of people slept in each room. There wasn't any food. A lot of men died from illness* or infection*. Florence changed everything. Soon the hospital was clean, and there was **7** .... to eat. She walked around the hospital for hours at night, always with her lamp.

Florence saved thousands of lives. People from different **8** .... followed her ideas, and more and more women wanted to be nurses.

Florence was often ill, but she was ninety years old when she died. Today, people still read her books about nursing. There are also 'Florence Nightingale' hospitals in many different countries.

3 Life was not easy for nurses during the Crimean war. Florence is talking to a new nurse. Complete her sentences with *must* or *mustn't*.

2 You .... clean the floors every day.

4 You .... give the men their food.

5 You .... go out to parties.

1 You ....must....... work hard.

3 You .... drink alcohol*.

6 You .... wash the men's wounds*.

7 You .... wear dirty clothes.

8 You .... be good at all times.

9 You .... always wash your hands.

10 You .... sleep when you are working.

4 Join the sentence halves in the lamps to learn more about Florence. Write the sentences.

1 Florence never had
2 Florence was in bed for
3 Florence wrote letters to
4 International* Nurses' Day is
5 When Florence arrived in the Crimea
6 There is a Florence Nightingale Museum
7 Florence's aunt*, Mai Smith
8 Three hospitals in Turkey

a a husband.
b on Florence's birthday.*
c the last 14 years of her life.
d the doctors did not want to see her.
e have the name 'Florence Nightingale'.
f in Saint* Thomas's Hospital in London.
g all the families of the dead soldiers.
h was also a nurse in the Crimea.

1 Florence never had a husband.
2 ....
3 ....
4 ....
5 ....
6 ....
7 ....
8 ....

Personal Project

- Did your country have any famous doctors or nurses in the past? What did they do?
- Choose one of them and find out more about him or her.

*What is it in your language? Find out!

Elizabeth Fry: a life of good work

1 Match the words and pictures with their meanings.

1 blanket

2 cell

3 to sew

a a building to keep bad people in ....prison........

b to make clothes by hand ....

c to kill someone with a rope round their neck ....

d to take something without asking or paying for it ....

e you put this over you to keep warm in bed ....

f this man or woman stops prisoners from leaving prison ....

g a room in prison for a prisoner to stay in ....

4 prison

2 Read the text on page 33 and write *True* or *False*?

1 Elizabeth Fry had three children. ....False........

2 She visited women in prison. ....

3 Each woman prisoner had her own room. ....

4 Elizabeth believed in helping prisoners to start new lives. ....

5 She believed in hanging. ....

6 She helped homeless people. ....

7 She went to the Crimea with Florence Nightingale. ....

8 Queen Victoria didn't help Elizabeth. ....

5 to steal

6 to hang

7 guard

Elizabeth Fry: 1780-1845

Elizabeth was the daughter of a Quaker banker. Quakers are Christians*. They believe in a simple* church, and they believe in helping poor people. In 1800 Elizabeth married Joseph Fry, a London merchant*. They had eight children, but Elizabeth still helped the poor. She was interested in prisoners.

Prisoners often became ill in prison at that time. When Elizabeth first visited Newgate (the biggest London prison) she found 300 women and their children in four cells. Prisoners slept on the floor without nightclothes or blankets. Women cooked, washed, and slept in the same cell. Elizabeth went back the next day with food and clothes.

In 1816 Elizabeth started a school for prisoners' children. She also taught women prisoners to read and sew. She wanted them to get jobs and start new lives when they came out of prison. She visited different prisons in Britain, and she talked to people in the British government*. Slowly British prisons became better. By the 1820s she was famous for her prison work.

At that time the British hanged people for stealing clothes or food. Elizabeth thought this was wrong and tried to stop hanging. Elizabeth also helped people with no homes. In 1840 she started a London school for nurses. Fry nurses were very good. Florence Nightingale took some of them with her to help in British hospitals in the Crimean War. Queen Victoria was interested in Elizabeth's work and gave her money to help her. When Elizabeth died, thousands of poor people were very sad.

3 Where can you see a picture of Elizabeth Fry today? Complete the sentences and find out.

1 Before Elizabeth Fry changed things, prisoners slept _o n_ the floor.

2 The second letter of 'hanging' is __

3 Two and three are __ __ __ __

4 The money in Britain is the __ __ __ __ __ .

5 One day Elizabeth left a __ __ __ __ for her husband at home.

It said 'I've gone to Newgate.'

Answer:

_on_ ....

....

4 Write –ed or –ing to complete the adjectives.

1 Elizabeth was interest_ed_ in helping people.

2 She didn't have a bor.......... life. It was full of activity.

3 She was sometimes tir.......... because she was busy.

4 She had some excit.......... ideas about changing prisoners' lives.

5 Queen Victoria thought Elizabeth's work was interest.......... .

6 The prisoners were bor.......... until she taught them to sew and read.

7 When she started her new school, she felt excit.......... .

8 Some of her days were very long and tir.......... .

Personal Project

- Which famous people have appeared on your country's money or its stamps?
- Find out more about one of them.

* What is it in your language?
Find out!

Votes for women

1 Answer these questions.

1 How old must you be to vote in your country?
2 Can women vote?
3 When did they get the vote?

In Britain, as in other countries, women had to fight to get the vote.

2 Look at the 'Women's Votes' timeline and answer the questions.

1 When did ordinary men get the vote in Britain?
.... 1832 ....
2 When did women get the vote?
....
3 Who were more violent, the suffragists or the suffragettes?
....
4 What three violent things did the suffragettes do?
....
5 Who were these people?
  a Emmeline Pankhurst
....
  b Herbert Asquith
....
  c Emily Wilding Davison
....
  d Lady Astor
....
6 What did British women do during the First World War?
....

1832: Ordinary British men get the vote. The women don't!

1867: 1,499 people ask for votes for women. The British Parliament* says 'No'.

1897: A society* is started in London. They are 'suffragists' – people who want votes for women.

1903: Emmeline Pankhurst starts a society in Manchester. The women in it are called 'suffragettes'. They want votes for women too, but are more violent* than the suffragists.

1905: The suffragettes interrupt* a politician while he is speaking. They refuse to pay the fine*, and they go to prison.

1908: Herbert Asquith becomes Prime Minister*. He does not agree with votes for women.

1909: The suffragettes attack important buildings and break shop windows.

1910: November 19th (Black Friday). 120 people are arrested* at a 'Women's Votes' meeting. Many are hurt in fights with the police.

1913: The suffragettes become more violent. They destroy pictures in museums and burn down buildings. They go to prison and refuse to eat. Suffragette Emily Wilding Davison throws herself in front of the king's horse at the Epsom Derby (a big English horse race). She dies from her injuries.

1914: The First World War begins. British men go away to fight, so British women start working in offices, factories and farms.

1918: The War ends. British women over 30 are given the vote. Things are happening!

1919: Lady Astor becomes the first British woman MP (Member* of Parliament).

1928: All British women over 21 are given the vote – at last!

1969: All British men and women over 18 are given the vote.

3 There are five scrambled words in the text. Read it and unscramble them.

The Cat and Mouse Act

Many of the suffragettes who went to prison went on 'hunger strike' –
they stopped eating. To keep the women **1** (evali) ....alive..... , the
British Government made a new law. People called it 'The Cat and
Mouse Act' because it was like a cat playing with a mouse before
it **2** (lilsk) .... it. Under this law, when a woman was on
hunger strike, prison doctors could put a rubber tube* into her
3 (umhot) .... and give her food through it. If a
woman became ill, she was sent home. When she was well
again, she had to go back to prison. Emmeline Pankhurst
was in prison **4** (eltvew) .... times in 1912
because of this act! To avoid the Cat and Mouse Act,
some women left England and went **5** (odaarb)
.... Christabel Pankhurst, Emmeline's
daughter, went to Paris.

4 What did they say? Write the verbs in the sentences.

1 If they ..don't give.. (not, give) us the vote, we 'll break......... (break) lots of windows. (Emmeline Pankhurst)

2 If these women .... (not, eat), we .... (make) them eat! (a prison doctor)

3 I .... (not/be) happy if they .... (not give) us the vote soon. (a suffragist)

4 If we .... (not get) the vote, I .... (jump) in front of the King's horse! (Emily Wilding Davison)

5 Those women .... never .... (receive) the vote if they .... (act) so stupidly. (Herbert Asquith)

6 If my wife .... (go) to prison, I .... (be) very upset. (the husband of a suffragette)

7 I .... (die) if I .... (not/eat) something soon. (a suffragette in prison)

8 If I .... (become) an MP, I .... (get) votes for women. (Lady Astor)

9 The world .... (be) a worse place if women .... (get) the vote. (The *Daily Mail* Newspaper)

10 If I .... (have to) go to prison again, I .... (run) away. (Christabel Pankhurst)

5 Did you know?
There was one place in Britain where women got the vote sooner – in 1881. It's an island.
Take out the people's names and find the name of the place.

emmelinepankhursttheherbertasquithisleemilywildingdavisonofladyastormanchristabelpankhurst

Personal Project
- Do ordinary men in your country have the vote? Since when? What about women?
- Find out more about the history of voting in your country.

* What is it in your language? Find out!

They cared for poor workers

1 Match the words in the bar of chocolate with their meanings.

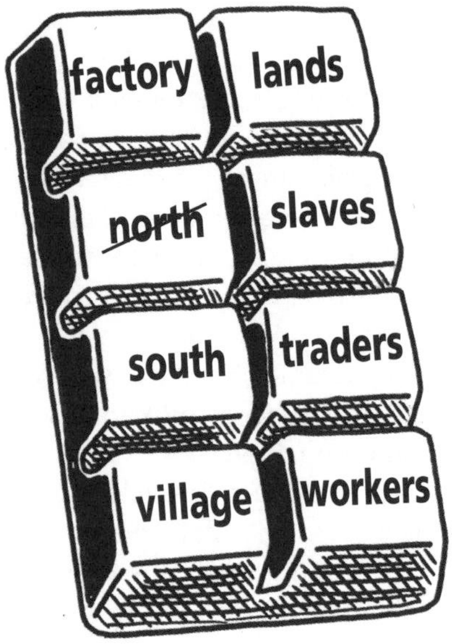

1 the opposite of south n o r t h

2 these people buy and sell things _ _ _ _ _ _ _

3 countries _ _ _ _ _ _

4 these people work for a rich person without pay _ _ _ _ _ _

5 a small town _ _ _ _ _ _ _

6 these people work for somebody _ _ _ _ _ _ _

7 people make things in this building _ _ _ _ _ _ _

8 the opposite of north _ _ _ _ _

factory	lands
north	slaves
south	traders
village	workers

2 Complete the text about William Wilberforce with words 1–4 from activity 1. Complete the text about George Cadbury with words 5–8.

William Wilberforce (1759-1833)

This isn't right!

William Wilberforce came from a rich family in Hull – in the **a** ....north.... of England. He had many important friends. One of them was the Prime Minister* William Pitt. When Wilberforce was 21 he became a Member of Parliament.*

In those days rich people in Britain had **b** .... to do work for them. Slave **c** .... bought and

sold people. They went to Africa. They put poor African people onto their boats and took them back to England. They sold them to rich white people there. Some boats took black slaves to the West Indies and North America. These countries were British **d** .... at the time. Many slaves died on the way.

From 1785, Wilberforce worked hard to stop the slave traders. In 1807, the British Parliament made a law* to stop people buying and selling slaves. But rich white people in the West Indies didn't care about the British law. They wanted cheap workers. Slave traders still sold black slaves to them.

Just before Wilberforce died, the British Parliament made a new law. It stopped people keeping slaves in all British lands.

George Cadbury (1839-1922)

George Cadbury and his family made chocolate. They had a small chocolate **e** .... in Birmingham. George was a good man. He talked to the **f** .... in his factory and he listened to their problems. Many rich people said, 'Poor people don't want to work. They like living in small, dirty houses!' George Cadbury didn't believe this, so he decided to help his workers.

Cadbury opened a new factory at Bourneville. It was in the country, **g** .... of Birmingham. Near the new factory there was a **h** .... with new houses in it for the workers. They were small houses but they were clean. Every house had a garden. It was a great idea. The workers at the Bourneville factory worked better because they were happier there.

People came from different countries to visit Bourneville. Soon, houses for workers got better in many other places. And today Cadbury's chocolate is famous around the world!

3 Read the texts about Wilberforce and Cadbury again. Correct the false words in these sentences.

1 William Wilberforce came from ~~Birmingham.~~ ....Hull.............

2 He worked hard to help slave traders. ....

3 The British Parliament made a law to stop people buying and selling sugar. ....

4 Just after Wilberforce died, a new law stopped people keeping slaves. ....

5 George Cadbury came from Hull. ....

6 He had a sugar factory. ....

7 He didn't listen to his workers. ....

8 Workers at Bourneville had dirty little houses. ....

4 Look at these sentences. Complete the rules with *so* or *because*.
Cadbury did not believe this, **so** he decided to help his workers.
     this came first ➡️ this came second
They worked better, **because** they were happier.
   this came second ⬅️ this came first

Rules
1 the word .... answers the question 'what happened next?'
2 the word .... answers the question 'why?'

5 Complete these sentences with *so* or *because*.

1 Cadbury wanted to help ....*so*........ he gave his workers better houses.

2 Cadbury's chocolate is famous .... it's good.

3 It was a long way to America .... many slaves got ill and died.

4 People wanted slaves .... they were cheap workers.

5 Wilberforce died happy .... the law stopped people keeping slaves.

6 Wilberforce came from a rich family .... his money helped him.

Personal Project
- Did any famous people help poor workers in your country? How did they do this?
- Choose one of these people and find out more about them.

* What is it in your language?
Find out!

They helped young people

1 Discuss these questions. What do you think?

1 What are the 'Boy Scouts'?
2 When did the 'Boy Scouts' start?
3 Why did the 'Boy Scouts' start?
4 Who started the 'Boy Scouts'?
5 How many countries have Boy Scouts today?

2 Read the text quickly and find answers to the questions.

3 Match the underlined words in the text with their meanings.

1 this group of people fights for their country on land

ⓐ r m y

2 guarded from attack __ _○_ _ _ _ _

3 different countries fight together in this __ _○

4 the most important __ _○_ _

5 people or animals leave these signs when they walk

in the country _ _ _ _○_

6 started to fight suddenly ○_ _○_ _ _ _

7 this is a beautiful, expensive precious stone

_ _ _ _ _○_

8 these people go in front of an army to bring back

news ○_ _ _ _ _

4 What language – close to Dutch – do Boers speak? Write the letters in the circles in order to find it.

A _ _ _ _ _ _ _ _ _

Lord* Baden Powell (1847-1941)

When Robert Baden Powell was 19, he went into the British <u>army</u>. They sent him to South Africa during the Boer <u>War</u>. The Boers were people from Holland. They didn't like the British taking their land in Africa. (There were <u>diamond</u> mines* there!) So they started a war against Britain.

One of Baden Powell's jobs in South Africa was to work with black African <u>scouts</u>. He taught them to understand <u>tracks</u> in the grass, and other things. In 1899 he wrote a book about scouting for them.

In 1900 the Boers <u>attacked</u> the town of Mafeking. Baden Powell <u>defended</u> the town against them. He had only 1,251 men and the Boers had 9,000. But Baden Powell defended Mafeking for 271 days until help arrived.

When Baden Powell went back to Britain, he was surprised. Lots of English boys liked his book on scouting! He wrote a new book *Scouting for Boys* for them in 1907, and started the 'Boy Scouts' in 1908. Baden Powell was the <u>Chief</u> Scout. He became Lord Baden Powell in 1929. There are Scouts in over 76 countries in the world today.

5 Write questions in the past about Baden Powell using these words.

1 what/do/when/be/19? ___What did he do when he was 19?___ ___He went into the British army.___

2 where/they/send him? ....

3 who/work with/there? ....

4 which town/the Boers/attack/in 1900? ....

5 how many men/Baden Powell/have? ....

6 how long/defend/the town? ....

7 when/start/the 'Boy Scouts'? ....

8 what/become/in 1929? ....

6 Read the text again and answer your questions.

7 Read about Lord Shaftesbury. Mark the sentences below T (true) or F (false).

Lord Shaftesbury (1801-1885)

Lord Shaftesbury came from a rich family, but he was an unhappy child. He hated school. When he was older he went into Parliament* and he did a lot to help poor people.

At the time many poor children had to work for very little money and in the poorest, dirtiest jobs. Some worked cleaning chimneys*, others worked in mines. Shaftesbury helped stop this.

Young children didn't have to work any more. They went to school to learn. Shaftesbury also helped to get a ten-hour working day. (Before that, some people worked all day and night!)

Shaftesbury Avenue* in London gets its name from this great man.

And when did you start in this job?

When I was five.

1 He came from a poor family. ___F He came from a rich family.___

2 He was a happy child. ....

3 He went into Parliament. ....

4 He did nothing to help poor people. ....

5 He helped children to find work. ....

6 He brought in a ten-hour day for workers. ....

Personal Project
- Did any famous people help children in your country? What did they do?
- Choose one of these people and find out more about him or her.

* What is it in your language? Find out!

Famous fighters

1 Use the clues to complete the crossword with the words from the box.

admiral battle captain ~~cathedral~~ invade telescope victory

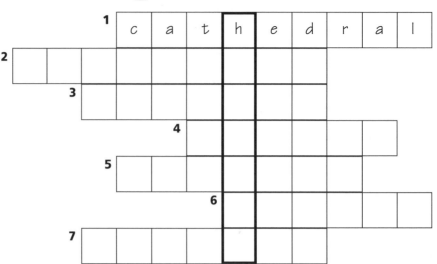

1. | c | a | t | h | e | d | r | a | l |

1 a big, important church

2 when you look through this, far things seem near

3 an important officer in the navy*

4 a big fight

5 the most important person on a ship

6 when fighters go into a country to win that country

7 the moment when you win a war

2 What was Admiral Nelson's first name? Find it in the completed crossword.

H _ _ _ _ _ _

Admiral Nelson (1758–1805)

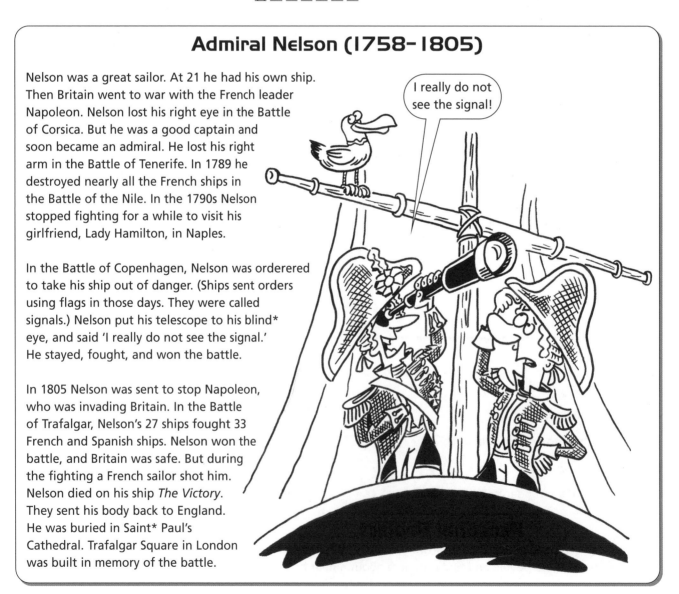

Nelson was a great sailor. At 21 he had his own ship. Then Britain went to war with the French leader Napoleon. Nelson lost his right eye in the Battle of Corsica. But he was a good captain and soon became an admiral. He lost his right arm in the Battle of Tenerife. In 1789 he destroyed nearly all the French ships in the Battle of the Nile. In the 1790s Nelson stopped fighting for a while to visit his girlfriend, Lady Hamilton, in Naples.

In the Battle of Copenhagen, Nelson was orderered to take his ship out of danger. (Ships sent orders using flags in those days. They were called signals.) Nelson put his telescope to his blind* eye, and said 'I really do not see the signal.' He stayed, fought, and won the battle.

In 1805 Nelson was sent to stop Napoleon, who was invading Britain. In the Battle of Trafalgar, Nelson's 27 ships fought 33 French and Spanish ships. Nelson won the battle, and Britain was safe. But during the fighting a French sailor shot him. Nelson died on his ship *The Victory*. They sent his body back to England. He was buried in Saint* Paul's Cathedral. Trafalgar Square in London was built in memory of the battle.

3 Read the text about Nelson. Complete these sentences with the correct names.

1 Nelson lost an eye at a sea battle near the French island of C o r s i c ⓐ.

5 Nelson died in the ⓒⓒ _ _ _ _ _ _ _Ⓞ_ _ _ _ _ _ _ .

2 Nelson lost an arm while he was attacking the French on the island of _ _ _ _ _Ⓞ_ _ _ .

3 Nelson destroyed nearly all the French ships in the _ _ _ _ _Ⓞ _ _ _ _ _ _ _Ⓞ_ .

4 In the _ _ _ _ _ _ ⓒⓒ _ _ _ _ _ _ _ _ _ _ _ Nelson did not follow orders.

6 Nelson's ship was the _ _ _ _ _Ⓞ_ .

7 Nelson was buried in _ _ _ _ _ _ _Ⓞ_ '_ _ _ _ _ _ _ _ _ .

8 Nelson's girlfriend was _ _ _ _ _ _Ⓞ_ _ _ .

4 What did they put Nelson's body in to take it to England?
Put the letters in circles in activity 3 in order to find out.

a _ _ _ _ _ _
_ _ _ _ _

5 Read the text about Wellington.
Complete these sentences with the correct names.

1 Napoleon escaped from the island of E l ⓑa .

2 Napoleon didn't escape from the island of ⬜_ _ ⬜ _ _ _ _ _ ⬜.

3 In 1815 Wellington won the Battle of _ _⬜_ _ _ⓒⓒ.

4 Napoleon lost the war against _ _ _ _⬜_ in 1814.

5 Britain sent an army to help the _ _ _Ⓞ_ _ _ _ _ _ and Ⓞ_ _ _ _ _ _ fight Napoleon.

6 Wellington's cleverest enemy was _ _ _ _ _ _ _⬜⬜ .

The Duke of Wellington (1769-1852)

When Napoleon invaded Spain and Portugal, Britain sent their best general, Wellington, to Portugal with a big army. They wanted to help the Portuguese and Spanish people.

In 1812 Napoleon sent most of his army to invade Russia. Wellington attacked the French who were still in Spain and they soon went back to France. In 1814 Napoleon lost the war against Russia. He was sent to the island of Elba.

When Napoleon escaped from Elba, Wellington went to attack him. In 1815, in the Battle of Waterloo in Belgium, Napoleon fought Wellington and lost. Napoleon was sent to the island of Saint Helena. He did not escape this time. Wellington returned to Britain and was made a Duke.

6 Use the letters in circles and squares in activity 5. Complete the sentence in the picture of Wellington.

Two things in Britain are named after me and my most famous battle:

Wellington

ⓄⓄⓄⓄⓄ

and

Waterloo

⬜⬜⬜⬜⬜⬜⬜ !

Personal Project

- Were there any famous army or navy fighters in your country? What battles did they win or lose?
- Find out more about one of them.

* What is it in your language? Find out!

The great fire of London

Imagine your house is on fire. What are you going to do? Phone the firemen of course! Now imagine you live in London in 1666. Your house is on fire. What are you going to do? There aren't any telephones, and there aren't any firemen. Help!

1 Can you guess the answers in the quiz?

The Great Fire of London Quiz

1 How many people lived in London in 1666?
   a) 600,000   **b)** 1 million   **c)** 2 million

2 How many people lost* their houses in the fire?
   a) 20,000   **b)** 100,000   **c)** 300

3 How many churches* burned* down?
   a) 10   **b)** 45   **c)** 89

4 How many people died?
   a) 500   **b)** 6   **c)** 2,000

5 How long did the fire burn?
   a) 2 weeks   **b)** 10 days   **c)** 4 days

Fire facts

The Great Fire of London in 1666 started on 2nd September and finished on 6th September. The number of people living in London at that time was 600,000 and about one sixth of them lost their houses. Many buildings burned down. London lost more than 87 churches, including the beautiful old cathedral* of Saint* Paul's. The fire was very bad but only 6 people lost their lives. The cost of the fire was about 30 million euros. (London made about 18,000 euros a year at this time.)

2 Read the text on the right and check your ideas.

3 Use the words in the bread to complete the diary.

expensive clothes
shouted window
frightened cakes

Diary of Thomas Farrinor, a baker

3rd September 1666

Yesterday I worked hard all day, making 1 .....cakes..... for King Charles II. At one o'clock in the morning, my wife

2 .... , 'Tom! Tom! The house is on fire!' It was true! The hot, angry fire was in all the rooms. Everyone

was very 3 .... In minutes the next house was on fire too. I shouted to the children and they came into

our bedroom. There was only one answer. One by one, we jumped out of the 4 .... into the street.*

Our poor maid Susannah cried. She said, 'I'm frightened! I can't jump!' It was so sad. She died in the fire.*

We ran to the river. I tried to get a cart but they were very 5 .... They cost £30! (50 euros.)*

At the river, there were hundreds of people in boats. We found a boat and started to leave. People watched

the fire from the river and cried. Everything was on fire – all the houses, churches and other buildings.

Saint Paul's cathedral came down as we watched.

We've got some money. But we haven't got a house. And we haven't got any 6 ....

What are we going to do now?

3 Your house is on fire. You've got only a few minutes. What five things do you take with you? Complete the words. Then tick the boxes.

1 my ph__tos ☐   **2** my CDs ☐   **3** some books ☐   **4** my n__w trainers ☐ **5** my mobile pho__e ☐

6 my computer ☐   **7** my comics ☐   **8** some chocolate ☐   **9** my ca__era ☐   **10** my diar__ ☐

4 Many people took this with them when they ran from the Great Fire. What was it?   _ _ _ _ _
Put the missing letters in activity 3 in this order to find it.   9 1 5 4 10

5 Put these words in the correct places in the text below.

> beautiful   churches   ~~important~~
>   it   quickly   river

6 Pepys buried* two things in his garden before he left his house. Can you find them in the picture?

1 E H E C E S _ _ _ _ _ _ _

2 E N W I _ _ _ _ _

Not bad!

Pepys and Wren

Samuel Pepys (we say 'Peeps') was an
1 .important... man, and a famous writer. He
watched the fire from across the **2** ....
He wrote about people running away from the fire.

Christopher Wren was a famous English architect*.
After the fire, he made plans for a **3** ....
new city. King Charles II liked Wren's plans,
but people wanted to go back to their homes
4 .... There wasn't time to build*
everything again. So the king told Wren, 'Build
all the London **5** .... again.'
For 50 years, Wren did that. And he built a new
Saint Paul's Cathedral. You can see **6** ....
today. He did a very good job!

Personal Project
- Were there any terrible natural disasters in your
country's history? What happened?
- Choose one disaster and find out more about it.

* What is it in your language? Find out!

The Black Death

**The Black Death* was a horrible illness*. It came to Britain in 1348
and travelled across the country. It killed thousands of people.**

1 Read the text and draw the route of the Black Death on the map.

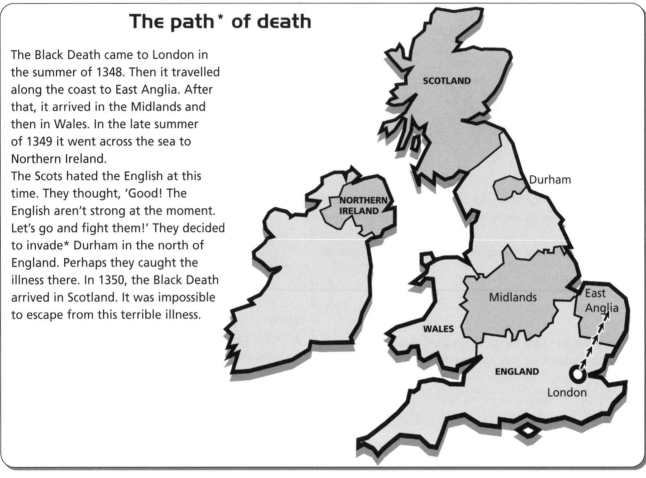

The path* of death

The Black Death came to London in
the summer of 1348. Then it travelled
along the coast to East Anglia. After
that, it arrived in the Midlands and
then in Wales. In the late summer
of 1349 it went across the sea to
Northern Ireland.
The Scots hated the English at this
time. They thought, 'Good! The
English aren't strong at the moment.
Let's go and fight them!' They decided
to invade* Durham in the north of
England. Perhaps they caught the
illness there. In 1350, the Black Death
arrived in Scotland. It was impossible
to escape from this terrible illness.

2 Write the words from the rat in the correct places in the table.

Signs of the illness	Causes*	Treatment*
headache		

3 What was the real cause and the best treatment?
Read the text on the next page and check your ideas.

1 The real cause was

....

2 The best treatment was

....

~~headache~~
God was angry   fever*
coughing* up blood   eating grass
touching an ill person   drinking bad water
rats   swellings* on the body
taking blood from the ill person
killing cats and dogs
leaving the cities
bad air*

The signs of illness

The ill person felt tired and had a headache and fever. They had swellings under their arms and on other parts of their body. Then they started to cough blood. They usually died about three days later.

What was the cause? For many years, nobody knew the real cause. People had different ideas:

'God is angry with the world and he wants to show us that.'
'Don't touch the ill people. They will give us the illness too!'
'Don't drink the water. It's bad!'
'The air is bad! Put something over your face!'
'It's the rats! They're bringing the illness into our streets and houses!'

It wasn't exactly the rats. The fleas* on the rats were the real cause. They carried germs*. When a rat died, the fleas looked for a new place to live. They jumped onto cats, dogs and, of course, people!

What was the treatment? People tried everything to stop the illness. They ate strange things like grass and made horrible drinks. Some doctors said, 'This illness is in the blood!' And they took blood from the ill person's body. Some people killed their cats and dogs. They believed the illness came from them. The best idea was to escape from the towns and cities, and go into the country. But only rich people could do that. Poor people had to stay in their houses.

The Great Plague*

The Black Death was terrible. About half the people of London died in the 1340s because of the Black Death. But the illness didn't disappear. In 1665 it came back to London. This time people called it, 'The Great Plague.'
When a family got the plague, people drew a cross on the front door of their house. Carts went around the city, and the driver shouted, 'Bring out your dead.' Then he took the dead bodies away.
One third of the people in London died of the plague between 1665 and 1666.
Now we know the cause of the illness and we can fight it. But in some parts of the world, the plague has not disappeared. It is still killing people today.

4 Read the texts about the Black Death and the Great Plague again. Answer these questions.

1   When did the Black Death first come to London?   ......in 1348......

2   When did it arrive in Scotland?   ....

3   How long did it usually take to kill someone?   ....

4   How many people in London died of it in the 1340s?   ....

5   What did people call the illness in 1665?   ....

6   How many people in London died of it between   ....
    1665 and 1666?

Personal Project
- Were there any terrible illnesses in your country in the past? Why did people get them? What were the cures?
- Choose one past illness and find out more about it.

* What is it in your language? Find out!

The Titanic

The *Titanic* was a huge ship, about the length of three football fields. Everyone was very proud of the *Titanic*. They thought it was the best ship in history - and the safest. Nobody could imagine the terrible accident that was going to happen.

1 Read some things that people said about the *Titanic*. Who was speaking <u>after</u> the accident?

> 'I have never been in an accident of any kind. I cannot imagine anything which could make a ship <u>sink</u> in our day. Modern shipbuilding has gone beyond that.'
> E. J. Smith, Captain of the *Titanic*

> 'God himself cannot not sink this ship.'
> A <u>crew</u> member*

> 'The Captain can, by simply moving an electric switch, <u>instantly</u> close the doors and make the ship <u>practically</u> impossible to sink.'
> the Shipbuilder magazine

> 'It was a beautiful ship. It was really a <u>floating</u> palace.'
> Edith Haisman, 15, a passenger

2 Match the underlined words with their meanings.

1 staying on top of the water   ....floating...........

2 almost   ....

3 go down under the water   ....

4 the people who work on a ship   ....

5 immediately   ....

Which two words are opposites?

to _ _ _ _ _ and to _ _ _ _

3 What do you think happened? Mark the sentences True or False. Then read the text and check your ideas.

1 The *Titanic's* first voyage* was from Britain to America.   ......True......

2 The ship hit another boat.   ....

3 There weren't enough lifeboats* for all the passengers.   ....

4 A lot of people refused to leave the ship.   ....

5 Fewer than half the people died.   ....

6 The *Titanic* was rescued and made more voyages.   ....

A terrible tragedy

The *Titanic* left England for New York on April 12th 1912. It had a crew of 892 people and 1,316 passengers. On April 14th, the crew saw an iceberg* in front of them. It was too late to do anything. The ship hit the iceberg, and the *Titanic* began to go down. There were 20 lifeboats on the Titanic, but 63 were needed to save everyone. However, not all the lifeboats were full. A lot of people stayed on the ship instead of trying to escape. They were sure that the *Titanic* could not sink. Only 650 people escaped in the lifeboats. Other people jumped into the sea when the boat went down. The sea was very cold and only 55 people survived it. A total of 705 people survived the terrible tragedy*. The *Titanic's* first voyage was also its last.

The night the *Titanic* sank

From a high place on the ship, Fred Fleet, a crew member, saw the iceberg just a few hundred metres away. He rang the bell* to warn* the people driving the ship. But it was travelling too fast to stop, and it hit the iceberg. Soon after that, one passenger, Major Peuchen, noticed that the ship wasn't straight in the water. But nobody listened to him.

Before the accident, the *Titanic* had received an ice warning. Another ship – the *Californian* – was about 30 kilometres north of the *Titanic*. When the *Californian* saw the iceberg, it stopped. It also sent a radio message to warn other ships in the area. At about 11.15, the *Californian's* radio operator* turned off the radio, and went to bed. The *Titanic* sent a message back giving its position - wrongly! The accident happened at about 11.40.

Soon after midnight, the crew of the *Californian* saw rockets going up into the sky from the *Titanic*. Their Captain said, 'Fireworks! The passengers of the *Titanic* are having a party.' The radio wasn't turned on again, and the *Californian* didn't move. At 12.25 am on the *Titanic*, people began to get into the lifeboats.

At 2.20 am on April 15th the *Titanic* finally sank. Another ship, the *Carpathia*, heard the *Titanic's* last call for help. It was 58 miles away, but it raced to help the ship. At 4.10 am, the *Carpathia* saw the *Titanic's* lifeboats floating on the dark water, and rescued the survivors*. Later, the *Californian* turned the radio back on, and heard that the *Titanic* had sunk.

4 Read the text above and put the sentences in order.

a A passenger noticed that the ship wasn't straight. (H)

b The *Carpathia* rescued the people in the lifeboats. (O)

c The crew of the *Californian* saw rockets in the sky. (M)

d The *Titanic* sent rockets into the sky. (A)

e There was an investigation into the accident. (N)

f Fred Fleet saw the iceberg and rang the bell. (U)

g The *Californian* turned off its radio. (O)

h Passengers began to get into the lifeboats. (P)

i The *Californian* sent a radio ice warning. (S) 1

j The *Titanic* hit the iceberg. (T)

k The *Titanic* finally sank. (T)

5 Put the letters in the lifebelts in order to make the name of an English town.

The *Titanic* sailed from here on its only voyage.

S _ _ _ _ _ _ _ _ _

Personal Project

- Were there any terrible accidents, or were any terrible mistakes made by people in your country in the past? What happened?
- Choose one accident or mistake and find out more about it.

* What is it in your language? Find out!

The wars of the roses

1 Read the text and colour the flags.

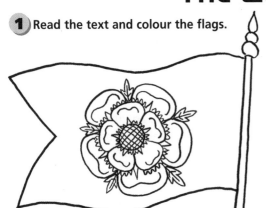

1 The House of York

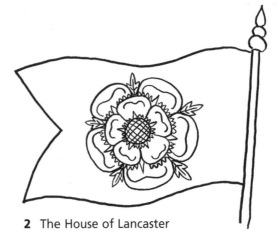

2 The House of Lancaster

2 Match the underlined words in the text with their meanings.

1 to hit someone many times <u>f i g h t</u>

2 the sons of a king _ _ _ _ _ _ _ _

3 the son of your father's brother _ _ _ _ _ _ _

4 to become someone's husband or wife _ _ _ _ _ _

5 a building for bad people _ _ _ _ _ _ _

6 the brother of your mother or father _ _ _ _ _ _

Fighting families

In 1422 Henry VI became the King* of England. He wasn't a strong king. His <u>cousin</u> was a strong man, and wanted to be king. They started to <u>fight</u>. There were two important families in England at the time. They were the House of Lancaster, and the House of York. The Lancaster flag had a red rose on it. The York flag had a white rose on it. People from both these families wanted to be king. The Wars* of the Roses lasted* for 40 years.

In 1461 Lord* Warwick said, 'Enough!' He helped Edward of York to become King Edward IV. Then Warwick said, 'You must <u>marry</u> a French girl.' Edward said 'No.' (He wanted an English wife.) Warwick became angry. He tried to make Henry VI king again. (Poor Henry was in <u>prison</u> in the Tower* of London.) Things were very bad. Edward killed* Warwick. Then Henry died a few days later.

In 1483 Edward died. His 12-year-old son became Edward V. Young Edward and his brother had an <u>uncle</u>, Richard. Richard wasn't a very kind uncle. He put the two <u>princes</u> in prison in the Tower. They died there a month later. Did Richard kill them? We don't know for sure, but he probably did. He became King Richard III.

Not everyone liked Richard. Many wanted Henry Tudor as their king. He came from Wales, and from part of the Lancaster family. People from the Houses of Lancaster and York said, 'Yes! Henry can be king, but he must marry Elizabeth of York, the sister of the poor princes in the Tower.' Henry did this, and the two families stopped fighting.

In 1485 Henry killed Richard at the Battle* of Bosworth. He became Henry VII, and the Wars of the Roses finished.

Up with the House of York!

The Lancasters for ever!

3 Read the text again and answer these questions.

Who …

1 … was the king when the Wars of the Roses started? .... Henry VI ....

2 … helped Edward of York to become king? ....

3 … didn't want to marry a French girl? ....

4 … tried to make Henry VI king again? ....

5 … killed Warwick? ....

6 … probably killed the princes in the Tower? ....

7 … married the sister of the princes in the Tower? ....

8 … became Henry VII? ....

4 How do we say kings' names? Write the names in full with these words.

> fourth sixth fifth seventh ~~third~~

1 Richard III _Richard the Third_ **2** Edward IV .... **3** Edward V ....

4 Henry VI .... **5** Henry VII ....

5 Follow the rules. Complete these sentences with *a/an*, *the* or –.

1 Henry VI was not ......a...... strong king.

2 .... King Henry VI had a French wife.

3 Edward IV put Henry VI in .... prison.

4 Edward IV didn't want .... French wife.

5 .... Tower of London is very famous.

6 Richard III wasn't .... very nice man.

7 Edward V wasn't .... old man when he died.

8 Elizabeth of York was .... daughter of Edward IV.

Rules for using *a/an*, *the* or nothing before nouns

1 We use *the* when there is only one of something: *the House of York*.
But with named kings we say *King Richard*, not *the King Richard*.

2 We use *a/an* to talk about one of many different things (*an* comes before *a*, *e*, *i*, *o*, and *u*): *a young king*, *an old lord*

3 We use nothing when we talk about what we usually do in a place:
He's at school now. (ie, learning there)
I was at the school today. (eg, speaking to my son's teacher)
And in phrases like *I want to be king.* and before named kings.

Personal Projects

1 Were there any wars between important families in your country? What happened?
- Choose one of these wars and find out more about it.
2 What symbols* did different groups in your country use in the past? What do they mean?
- Find out more about one of them.

*What is it in your language? Find out!

The English civil war

1 Look at the text and complete the sentences with the correct names.

1 The Cavaliers were followers of .... **2** The Roundheads were followers of ....

King Charles I and Cromwell

In 1629 King Charles I closed Parliament.* 'I don't need it,' he said. For the next eleven years, he ruled* without it. But then he needed money for his <u>army</u>. In 1640 he called Parliament back, and asked for money. In the end, they said 'yes.' But many people were not happy with the king.

In 1641 Parliament said, 'We can rule without the king!' Charles got ready to <u>attack</u> London with an army of his followers. People on the side of Parliament got ready to fight the king. It was <u>Civil War</u>. Charles's followers were 'Cavaliers'. They had long hair and fine clothes.

Oliver Cromwell

Oliver Cromwell was the leader* on the side of Parliament. His followers were 'Roundheads'. They had very short hair and very ordinary clothes. Charles lost the war and went to Scotland for help. The Scots weren't happy with Charles, because he said 'no' to a free Scottish church. They gave him to Cromwell. In 1649 Parliament said, 'Charles I has <u>betrayed</u> his country.' They cut off his head.

After that, England became a country without a king. Cromwell became England's next ruler. He died in 1658, and his son Richard became the new ruler after him.

But Richard wasn't a strong man, and he couldn't pay the army. So they decided not to follow him. Suddenly there was fighting everywhere again. England needed a strong ruler once more.

Charles II was living in Holland at the time. He offered to pay the army, and to let the Scottish church be free. He also decided to forget about Parliament working against his father. But he couldn't <u>forgive</u> his father's killers.

Parliament decided to invite Charles back to England as the next king. England's days as a <u>republic</u> were over!

King Charles I

King Charles II

2 Match the underlined words in the text with their meanings.

1 a fight between two groups from the same country   <u>C i v i l   W a r</u>

2 a country without a king   _ _ _ _ _ _ _ _

3 to start fighting suddenly   _ _ _ _ _ _

4 to stop being angry with someone   _ _ _ _ _ _ _

5 these people fight for their country   _ _ _ _

6 broke a promise to   _ _ _ _ _ _ _ _

3 Read the text again and mark the sentences True or False.

		True	False
1	Charles I didn't like Parliament.	T ✓	C ☐
2	Charles I never needed money.	L ☐	H ☐
3	Charles I asked the Scots for help.	E ☐	U ☐
4	The Scots were happy with Charles.	R ☐	A ☐
5	In 1649 Charles I lost his head.	T ☐	C ☐
6	Oliver Cromwell became the King of England.	H ☐	R ☐
7	Richard Cromwell paid the army.	D ☐	E ☐
8	Charles II decided to forgive his father's killers.	Y ☐	S ☐

Did you know?

Charles II was a fun-loving king. He had lots of girlfriends. He met one of them - Nell Gwynn - when she was selling oranges in the street!

4 Put the correct letters in the boxes in activity 3 in order to complete this sentence.

Oliver Cromwell closed all the T _ _ _ _ _ _ _ in England when he was the leader of the country.

5 Correct Mike Mistake's history essay by writing the opposite of the underlined words. Use the words in Nell Gwynn's oranges to help you.

<u>Before</u> **1** .... After .... they cut off Charles's head, a lot of people were angry. After all, he was the <u>queen</u> **2** .... Some people became <u>poor</u> **3** .... by taking things from houses and churches. But the war was <u>cheap</u> **4** .... and after it, business was <u>good</u> **5** .... Working people began to <u>love</u> **6** .... Cromwell and his men. He <u>opened</u> **7** .... drinking houses. It was <u>possible</u> **8** .... to play football or dance on Sundays. Many ordinary men and women were very <u>happy</u> **9** .... with that. There was <u>a lot of</u> **10** .... fun in their lives under Cromwell. So lots of people <u>cried</u> **11** .... and sang when Charles II came back to England.

Personal Project

- Did your country lose its ruler or have a civil war at any time in its history?
- What happened? Find out more about it.

*What is it in your language? Find out!

Two world wars

1 These are posters from the First and Second World Wars. What did they say?

1 needs country YOU! Your

2 journey necessary? Is really your

3 costs Careless lives! talk

....

2 Match the underlined words in the two texts with their meanings.

1 shared between many people   ......*rationed*......

2 the son of your brother or sister   ....

3 this kills you, or makes you ill, if you smell or taste it ....

4 someone on your side in a war   ....

5 a paper that people sign to end a war   ....

6 these hang at windows and shut out the light   ....

7 a paper that people sign to show that they have the same opinion ....

The First World War (1914–1918)

In the 1910s the German leader, Kaiser Wilhelm II, built lots of ships. The British were worried that he wanted to attack them.

In 1914, a Bosnian Serb shot Franz Ferdinand, the <u>nephew</u> of the Austrian Emperor*. It was the start of the war: Austria and its <u>ally,</u> Germany, against Serbia and its allies, Russia and France. The Kaiser decided to attack France first by going through Belgium. When he had won, he planned to fight Russia. But Belgium is very close to Britain. The British asked the Kaiser to leave. He refused, so Britain sent an army* to France.

The generals* on both sides used heavy guns first, then they sent their foot soldiers to attack. But this was a modern war. Machine-guns, planes, and <u>poison</u> gas were used. Many thousands of men were killed.

In 1915 the Germans attacked the *Lusitania* – a British ship with American passengers on it. America joined the war against the Kaiser in 1917. The next year they sent an army to France.

The Kaiser tried to take Paris, but his tired German army met fresh American soldiers. On 11 November 1918 the Kaiser wanted to end the

war. Britain, America and France agreed to a <u>Peace Treaty</u> at Versailles, in France.

Kaiser Wilhelm II

The Second World War (1939–1945)

Adolf Hitler

In the 1930s the German leader Adolf Hitler moved into the Rhineland and Austria. Then he took Czechoslovakia. At first, Britain did nothing. They were more worried about Mussolini in Italy and Hirohito in Japan.

Then Hitler attacked Poland. He shared Poland with the Russian leader Josef Stalin. The British had an <u>agreement</u> with Poland so they told him to stop. Hitler refused and Britain entered the war.

A small British army went to France to fight Hitler's army. But the German army was stronger. The British left France in fishing boats.

The Second World War was very different from the First. Hitler's planes bombed* British cities and British planes bombed German cities. During the 'Blitz' (the German bomb attacks on London), people sent their children to the country because they were safer there. At night, people covered the windows with black <u>curtains</u> so Hitler's bombers couldn't see their targets*.

Food was <u>rationed</u>, and people grew their own vegetables. British women worked in all types of jobs while British men went off to fight.

The British Prime Minister* Winston Churchill spoke to the British people by radio during the war. This helped them to feel brave in difficult times.

In 1941 Hitler attacked Russia and the war started to go against him. At the end of 1941, America entered the war after Hirohito's attack on Pearl Harbour. In 1944 British, Canadian and American soldiers in France attacked Hitler on one side, while Russia fought against him on the other side. The Second World War in Europe finally ended in 1945.

Winston Churchill

3 Read the texts again. Tick these sentences World War One or World War Two.

		WW1	WW2
1	Hitler was the leader of Germany.	R ☐	(E) ☑
2	Churchill was the leader of Britain.	E ☐	V ☐
3	Franz Ferdinand of Austria was shot.	A ☐	F ☐
4	Kaiser Wilhelm II entered Belgium.	C ☐	U ☐
5	Japan attacked Pearl Harbour.	G ☐	U ☐
6	The British left France in fishing boats.	O ☐	E ☐
7	Germany and Russia shared Poland.	R ☐	E ☐
8	The Germans attacked the *Lusitania*.	S ☐	Y ☐

4 Put the letters next to the boxes you ticked in activity 3 in order to answer this question:
What name was given to British children who were sent away to the country during the Second World War?

E _ _ _ _ _ _ _

*What is it in your language? Find out!

5 Complete the text with the words in the box.

Britain   wear   flower   ~~Sunday~~   ended   soldiers

'Remembrance Day' is the nearest **1** Sunday. to the 11th November – the day the First World War **2** .... On that day many people in **3** .... are silent for two minutes and they **4** .... red poppies* on their jackets. They do this to remember all the **5** .... , sailors and pilots who died in the two World Wars. Why poppies? The poppy is a red **6** .... , the colour of blood. And there are poppies in many of the old World War I battlefields*.

Personal Project
- Was your country involved in past wars? Who were your country's enemies and allies? How do you remember the people who fought for your country?
- Find out more about one of these wars.

Three great writers

Geoffrey Chaucer (1345 –1400)

In Chaucer's day, there was no television, and there weren't many books. Most people couldn't read. What did they do? They told stories.

Chaucer's most famous book is *The Canterbury Tales*. (A tale is a story.) He wrote it in 1387. In the book, a number of people meet in London. Chaucer is one of them. The people are pilgrims*. They want to go to Canterbury to see the Shrine* of Saint* Thomas Becket. But it's far away. They decide to tell stories to make the time pass more quickly. Each pilgrim must tell two stories on the way to Canterbury, and two on the way back. There were 31 pilgrims, but there are only 23 stories in the book. Chaucer died before he finished it. Most of the stories are funny - and some are a bit rude*!

1 Read the text about Chaucer. Mark the sentences True or False. Correct the false sentences.

1 Chaucer lived about 300 years ago.   .... *False. He lived about 600 years ago.* ....

2 Not many people could read at that time.   ....

3 People liked telling stories in Chaucer's day. ....

4 The people in Chaucer's book met in London. ....

5 It wasn't far to Canterbury.   ....

6 Each pilgrim decided to tell four stories.   ....

7 Chaucer didn't finish the book.   ....

8 Most of the stories are sad.   ....

2 Match the pictures on the next page with the numbered parts of the text about Shakespeare.

William Shakespeare (1564–1616)

1 Shakespeare is Britain's most famous writer. Today, students around the world read his plays in different languages. But in Shakespeare's day people didn't read his plays, they went to see them at the theatre.

2 Shakespeare wrote his plays for one theatre company*, the Lord* Chamberlain's* Men. They were all men. Women couldn't act* in theatres in those days. Shakespeare acted for the Lord Chamberlain's Men, too.

3 They acted in the Globe Theatre, near the Thames in London. The theatre had no roof – so dry weather was important. Rich people had chairs to sit on. Poor people stood – and Hamlet was three hours long! People shouted and laughed, and sometimes they talked to the actors!

4 In 1613 there was a big fire in the Globe, but they built a second Globe Theatre in its place. In 1643 they closed this theatre to build houses. Today there is a new Globe Theatre in the same place. It is the same as Shakespeare's Globe. Some people stand and watch the plays – just like the people in Shakespeare's day.

a ....

Do I make a good Juliet?

b ....

Read that!

c ....

I know people stood in Shakespeare's Globe, but my feet hurt!

d ....

Be careful, Hamlet!

3 Read the texts about Chaucer, Shakespeare and Dickens. Tick the correct boxes.

WHO...	Chaucer	Shakespeare	Dickens
1 ...wrote Hamlet?	☐	☑	☐
2 ...acted in plays?	☐	☐	☐
3 ...wrote novels?	☐	☐	☐
4 ...worked when he was very young?	☐	☐	☐
5 ...lived for 52 years?	☐	☐	☐
6 ...went on a pilgrimage?	☐	☐	☐
7 ...is the most famous writer?	☐	☐	☐
8 ...didn't finish his best book?	☐	☐	☐

4 Complete each sentence with the *-ing* form of the correct verb.

> act (E)   be (I)   read (E)   ride (O)   see (T)   shout (U)
> sit (O)   stand (J)   ~~tell~~ (R)   work (L)   write (M)

1 People in Chaucer's time loved ...*telling*... stories.

2 The pilgrims enjoyed .... to Canterbury.

3 Chaucer didn't like .... sad stories.

4 Shakespeare loved .... in his plays.

5 Rich people liked .... on chairs at the Globe.

6 Poor people didn't enjoy .... at the theatre.

7 People loved .... at the actors.

8 Dickens hated .... in a factory.

9 Dickens' family hated .... in prison.

10 People loved .... Dickens' newspaper stories.

11 Dickens didn't like .... children at work in factories.

5 Put the letters after the verbs in activity 4 in order to find the name of a famous Shakespeare play.

R _ _ _ _ and _ _ _ _ _ _ _

Charles Dickens (1812–1870)

Charles Dickens is famous for his novels*. They are very long because he wrote them in different parts for a newspaper each week. Dickens' novels have a lot of exciting and sad things in them. He wanted his readers to buy the newspaper every week. And the readers wanted to finish the story!

In 1824 Dickens' father went to prison* because he couldn't pay money to someone. In those days, a man's wife and young children went to prison with him. Charles was 12, so he went to work in a factory*. Life was hard, and a lot of children worked in those days.

Dickens often wrote about poor children without a mother or father. His books *David Copperfield* and *Oliver Twist* are about boys without fathers. Important people were more interested in the problems of poor people after reading Dickens' books.

Personal Project
- Who were the greatest writers in your country? When did they live? What did they write?
- Find out more about one of them.

*What is it in your language? Find out!

Women writers

1 Read about Jane Austen. Four more sentences aren't true about Jane. Cross them out.

2 Read about George Eliot. Complete each sentence below with the correct name.

Jane Austen (1775-1817)

People love Jane Austen's novels. At this moment, there are probably a few thousand people reading one of them. ~~She worked in a burger bar when she wrote them.~~ A few more thousand are probably watching a DVD of one of her stories.

What did she write? Novels about women looking for husbands! Jane didn't write about politics* or things in other countries. She watched the people around her, and wrote about them. ~~She wore jeans a lot too.~~ A 'good marriage*' was important for a girl like her from a good family. Without a husband, a girl had to stay at home with her parents, or teach children in another family. ~~Jane drove a red sports car.~~

Jane was the daughter of a clergyman*. She had four brothers and a sister. She didn't have to worry about money, and people liked her books. ~~She used a computer to write her novels.~~

Did Jane find a good husband? No, she didn't. ~~She looked for one on the Internet.~~ A young man, Harris Bigg-Wither, wanted to marry her. At first she said 'Yes'. But the next day she said, 'No.' He wasn't the right person for Jane.

George Eliot (1819–1880)

'George' is usually a man's name. George Eliot's real name was Mary Ann Evans. Why did she use a man's name? A lot of women wrote love stories in those days. Some of these stories were a bit stupid. George was an intelligent woman and she wanted her books to be different.

In 1854, George went to live with another George (a man). This was terrible for many people because George Henry Lewes was already married. His wife refused to divorce him. The two Georges lived together until 1878 when Lewes died. Two years later, George Eliot married her friend John Cross. He was 20 years younger than her.

George Eliot had a more exciting life than Jane. She wrote for magazines, and she was interested in politics and changing things. She was a great writer, but her books didn't sell as well as Jane Austen's. They were longer and talked more about English politics. Today, you can see films of many of her novels. They are very popular.

1 George Eliot was really called ..Mary Ann Evans..

2 George Eliot lived with .... but she

   didn't marry him.

3 George Eliot married ....

4 George Eliot had a very different life from the writer,

   ....

3 Read about the Brontë sisters on the next page. Write the names they used when they wrote.

Charlotte Brontë   ....

Emily Brontë   ....

Anne Brontë   ....

The Brontë Sisters
Charlotte (1816–55), Emily (1818–48), Anne (1820–49)

The Brontë sisters lived in Yorkshire, in the north of England. Their father was a clergyman, like Jane Austen's, but their life was very different. Their mother died when they were little, and they went to a horrible boarding* school. When Charlotte, Emily and Anne started to write, they took men's names: Currer Bell, Ellis Bell and Acton Bell. (They kept the first letters of their real names!) Later, when their books were famous, they used their own names. All the sisters died young. Only Charlotte married – but she died soon after.

The novels of the Brontë sisters are dark and strange. They tell sad love stories about strong and difficult people - often living in big, scary houses in the hills. Today, there are films and songs about them. People still visit the Brontës' house today.

I don't just love Heathcliff. I am Heathcliff.

4 Who wrote what?
Read the clues. Which books belong to which writers?

1 Writer: ....
Adam Bede   Silas Marner
Middlemarch Daniel Deronda

2 Writer: ....
Persuasion*   Mansfield Park
Pride* and   Emma
Prejudice*

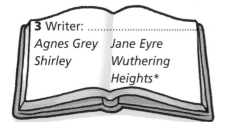

3 Writer: ....
Agnes Grey   Jane Eyre
Shirley   Wuthering
              Heights*

Clues: Jane Austen's books have the names of places, people, and feelings. Almost all the Brontës' books have the names of women. George Eliot's books have the names of men and places.

5 Read and complete the text about Austen, Eliot, and the Brontës with the correct verbs.

Most of the conversations in Jane Austen's books have women in them. She didn't **1** know (J) / work (V) how men talked when women weren't there! The only picture of Jane is in the National Portrait Gallery, a famous picture museum in London. Her sister Cassandra **2** threw (I) / drew (A) it.

George Eliot **3** wrote (N) / did (L) Middlemarch. It's about a small English town before people **4** got (E) / tried (L) the vote* in 1832. Many writers **5** went (S) / fell (E) in love with Eliot. One was the American writer, Henry James.

Two of the Brontë sisters – Charlotte and Emily – **6** worked (Y) / were (T) as teachers in England. Charlotte also **7** went (R) / came (T) to teach in Belgium. The Brontës' brother, Branwell, painted pictures of his three sisters. He **8** was (E) / went (R) in one of the pictures too. Later he painted over his face, leaving only the girls.

6 Write the letters after the correct verbs in activity 5 to find the name of Charlotte Brontë's most famous book.

....

Personal Project
- Were there any famous women writers in your country? When did they live? What did they write?
- Find out more about one of them.

*What is it in your language? Find out!

Romantic poets

Do you like poetry*? All these men were poets*.
They lived at a time of change in history. For example,
there were revolutions* in the United States, France
and Ireland. The Romantics wanted to change poetry.
They wanted more people to read and enjoy it.
They tried to use language that everyone
could understand.

Some of these poets were friends. Shelley and Byron
travelled to Switzerland and Italy together. Keats
lived in Rome for a time. Some of them were strange.
Byron, for example, was described as 'mad, bad and
dangerous to know!' All of them wrote great poetry.

The poems
Often, their poems had short lines, and they rhymed.
The words 'bright' and 'night' rhyme with each other
in this example:

Tiger, tiger burning bright,
In the forests of the night.
Blake

William Blake (1757–1827)
William Wordsworth (1770–1850)
Samuel Taylor Coleridge (1772–1834)
Lord Byron (1788–1824)
Percy Bysshe Shelley (1792–1822)
John Keats (1795–1821)

1 Read the text about the Romantic Poets.
Answer the questions

1 Who was born first? ...Wordsworth...

2 Who was born last? ....

3 Who was born in the 18th century? ....

4 Who died in the 19th century? ....

5 Who lived the longest? ....

6 Who died the youngest? ....

2 Choose two words that rhyme with the first word in
each group. Try saying the words with a partner.

a **night:** (bright) lit (white) wait

b **young:** sound sung tongue song

c **cage*:** page large age garage

d **side:** wide list said died

e **sea:** teach free be fear

f **now:** know how flower allow

g **men:** women pen end ten

3 Complete the poem with words that rhyme from
activity 2.

Romantic poets lived in an **1** ....*age*........

When lovely words were on the page.

Some died old, but most died **2** ....

Their poems now are rapped and sung.

One wrote about a man at sea.

These poets wanted to be **3** ....

They travelled Europe far and wide

Until the very day they **4** ....

Their names are famous even now.

Our English teachers don't **5** ....

Their students to forget these men.

Each changed our history with his **6** ....

The poets

Blake was good at imagining things. He also had 'visions'. (These are dreams that you have when you are awake.) He was an artist, and he drew pictures to go with his poems.

Keats died very young, but we can see his love of life and the natural world in his poetry. He looked for beauty in the things around him.

Alone, alone, all all alone,
Alone on a wide, wide sea.
The Ancient Mariner

Wordsworth was a rebel too when he was young, but he lived for many years. He lived in the Lake District, a beautiful area of mountains and lakes in the north-west of England. He wanted 'his' hills to be free of tourists. Today, his house in the Lake District is visited by thousands of tourists – the same kind of people that Wordsworth didn't like!

Byron was the most popular poet of his day. His poems were great and his life was exciting. The word 'Byronic' means someone who is romantic, handsome, free and a rebel*. Byron loved Greece, and he went to fight with them against Turkey, but he was ill on the boat and died on the way.

Shelley liked travelling and lived in other countries. He and his wife Mary met Byron in Italy. They enjoyed telling ghost stories. One of these stories gave Mary Shelley the idea for her fantastic book *Frankenstein*.

Coleridge was a friend of Wordsworth's. When he was young, he took opium* for pain in his teeth and head. Later, he couldn't stop taking it. He probably wrote some of his best poems while he was taking opium. He wrote a long poem about a sailor lost at sea: *The Ancient Mariner* (The Old Sailor.) It's full of strange and beautiful things. Today, it's one of his most popular poems.

4 Read the texts about Coleridge, Keats, Shelley, Byron and Wordsworth. Mark these sentences True or False.

1 The poets had boring lives. ....*False*..

2 They all lived in England. ....

3 They wrote for a very small group of people. ....

4 Blake could draw. ....

5 Coleridge had a drink problem. ....

6 Percy Shelley didn't write Frankenstein. ....

7 Keats hated nature. ....

8 Byron had an interesting personality. ....

9 Wordsworth was a rebel all his life. ....

10 The Lake District isn't popular ....
with tourists today.

*What is it in your language? Find out!

5 Rearrange the letters to find a fact that not many people know.
Byron's daughter, Ada Augusta Lovelace, wrote the world's first

– – – – – – – – – – – – – – – – – –

(POTECURM GRAPORM)

Personal Project
- Were there any groups of writers who started new fashions in writing in your country? When and where did they live? What did they write?
- Find out more about one of these groups.

They changed their world

1 Match the pictures with the words.

book ~~computer~~ printing press radio telephone television

1 .... *computer* .... 2 .... 3 ....

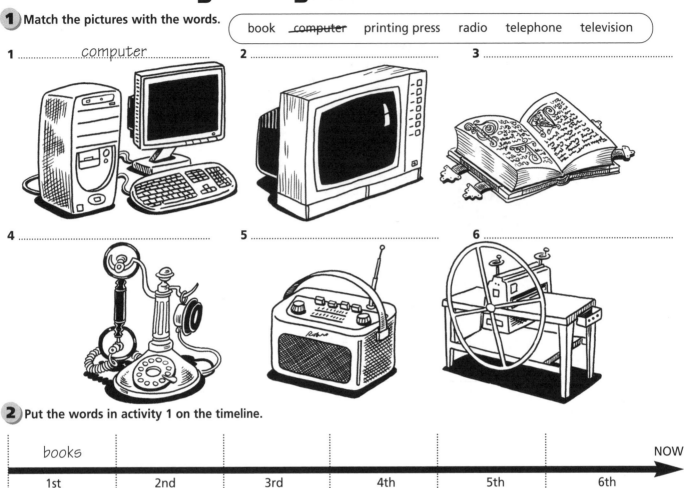

4 .... 5 .... 6 ....

2 Put the words in activity 1 on the timeline.

books   NOW

1st   2nd   3rd   4th   5th   6th

3 Look at the texts on the next page quickly. Match the people with the inventions.

1 Charles Babbage   **a** the telephone

2 John Logie Baird   **b** computer programs

3 William Caxton   **c** the computer

4 Ada Lovelace   **d** the television

5 Alexander Graham Bell   **e** the printing press

4 Read the texts again. Mark these sentences True or False.

1 Before the printing press, people copied books by hand. .... *True* ....

2 Caxton invented the printing press.   ....

3 Babbage didn't finish making the first computer.   ....

4 Babbage wrote the first computer program.   ....

5 Bell was English.   ....

6 Bell was a teacher of deaf people.   ....

7 The pictures on early TVs were very big.   ....

8 They sold a lot of TVs in Britain in the early fifties. ....

5 What do we call TV, radio, phones and the Internet together? Put the underlined letters in these names in the correct spaces to complete the word.

J<u>oh</u>n Logie Ba<u>ir</u>d

Alex<u>an</u>der Graha<u>m</u> Be<u>ll</u>

<u>C</u>harles Babbage

T _ L _ C _ M _ U _ I _ AT _ O _ S

Famous innovators*

William Caxton (1422–1491)

In 1469, Caxton translated* a French book into English. Lots of people in England wanted to read it. But in those days people copied* books by hand. That was very slow.

This isn't very quick.

Caxton heard about Gutenberg's printing press in Germany. 'That's a good idea!' he said. In 1476, Caxton started the first printing press in England. He used his press to make about 100 books. Geoffrey Chaucer's 'Canterbury Tales*' was one of them.

Charles Babbage (1792–1871)

Charles Babbage was a mathematician* at Cambridge University*. He wanted to find the answers to maths problems quickly. He started to make a special machine* to do this. Another mathemetician, Ada Lovelace, wrote the world's first computer program* for him. Babbage died before he finished his machine. But people still call him 'the grandfather of the computer'.

Maths will be easy with my machine!

Alexander Graham Bell (1847–1922)

Bell came from Scotland, but he later went to live in the USA. He made one of the first telephones there in 1876. The first telephone call was to Bell's assistant* in the next room. Bell said, 'Mr. Watson. Come here. I want to see you.' Bell also helped deaf* people to speak. He became American in 1882.

What does he want now?

John Logie Baird (1888–1946)

The British call John Logie Baird 'the father of television.' In 1926 people saw 'pictures by radio' for the first time on one of Baird's TVs. In 1936 the BBC (the first British television company*) started to broadcast.* The early TVs were very big, but the picture was small and in black and white. They weren't like today's televisions!

In 1953, lots of British people wanted a TV. They wanted to watch Elizabeth II's coronation* on it. They sold a lot of televisions in Britain that year!

Personal Project

- Were there any famous inventors from your country? Did they follow or use other inventors' ideas? What did they invent?
- Find out more about one inventor's life and inventions.

*What is it in your language? Find out!

They discovered it

1 Ask and answer these questions with a partner.

1 Have you ever been ill? What illnesses have you had?   2 Do you like having injections*? Why (not)?
3 Have you ever taken penicillin*? Why?   4 Have you ever been in hospital? Why?
5 Have you ever had an operation*? Why?

2 Read the text about Edward Jenner. Answer the questions in one word.

1 What was his job?   .... *doctor* ....

2 Which illness was worse – cowpox* or smallpox*?   ....

3 What did Jenner call his discovery?   ....

4 How do you say the Latin word 'vacca' in English?   ....

Edward Jenner (1749-1823)

In the past, many people died from smallpox. A lot of them were children. It was a very bad illness. Jenner wanted to find a way to stop people getting it. The answer was another illness – cowpox. Cowpox wasn't as bad as smallpox. And after someone had cowpox, they never caught smallpox. Jenner, a country doctor, learnt this from studying milkmaids*.

In 1796 Jenner injected a young boy with liquid* from a cowpox spot. The boy got cowpox, but after six weeks he was better. Then Jenner injected the same boy with liquid from a smallpox spot. The boy did not get ill! Jenner called this way of stopping people getting ill 'vaccination'. (Vacca is 'cow' in Latin.)

3 True or False? What do you think?

In the past ...

1 lots of people died after operations.   ....

2 doctors wore special clothes for operating.   ....

3 doctors didn't always wash their hands.   ....

4 doctors always cleaned their knives.   ....

Read the text about Joseph Lister. Were you right?

Joseph Lister (1827-1912)

When Joseph Lister became a doctor, many people got ill and died after they had operations. Why? Nobody was sure.

In those days, doctors didn't wear special clothes during operations. They didn't always wash their hands or clean their knives before operating.

Lister read about Louis Pasteur's work in France on germs*. In Lister's hospital doctors started to wear special clothes for operations. They washed their hands, and used clean knives when operating. Few people died after operations at his hospital after that.

I'm sure that there are lots of germs in this room!

Did you know?
Listerine® mouthwash gets its name from Joseph Lister.

4 Read the text about Alexander Fleming.
Cross out four more sentences that aren't correct.

Sir Alexander Fleming (1881–1955)

One day in 1928 Alexander Fleming, a Scot, was working in his laboratory* at Saint* Mary's Medical School in London. ~~He worked as a cleaner there.~~ He saw some green mould* on one of his laboratory dishes* and studied it carefully. He used his computer to do this. When germs came near the mould, it killed them. Fleming called his discovery 'penicillin'. He told everyone about it on TV the next day. But penicillin was expensive to make in those days.

In 1941 two men in Oxford – Henry Florey and Ernst Chain – found a cheaper way to make penicillin. They used mobile phones to talk to each other as they worked in different laboratories. In 1945 Fleming, Florey and Chain got a Nobel Prize* for their work. They made the computer game 'Penicillin' the next year.

Go on, Penicillin, kill those germs!

5 Read the texts again and mark these sentences J (Jenner), L (Lister) or F (Fleming).

1 He got a Nobel Prize for his work. ....F...........

2 He came from Scotland. ....

3 He worked in the country. ....

4 He worked at Saint Mary's Medical School. ....

5 He read about Louis Pasteur's work. ....

6 A mouthwash gets its name from him. ....

7 He was born in the eighteenth century. ....

8 He died in 1912. ....

Personal Project
- Did any men or women from your country discover anything important? What was it? How did it help the world?
- Find out more about one of them.

***What is it in your language?
Find out!**

Great thinkers

1 Match the words in the box with their meanings.

			box
1	animals such as gorillas	......*great apes*......	evolution
2	an idea about how something works	....	gravity
3	this makes far things look near	....	~~great apes~~
4	belonging to the king or queen	....	mint
5	the way that living things change to fit their homes better	....	royal
6	the place that makes a country's money	....	telescope
7	this stops the moon flying away into space	....	theory

2 Was it Darwin or Newton? Can you guess? Which great thinker realised...

1 ...that the earth has gravity? ......N.....

2 ...that animals change over time to match their homes? ....

3 ...that people and great apes are relatives? ....

4 ...that white light is made of different colours? ....

Read the texts quickly to check your ideas.

Charles Darwin (1809–1882)

When Darwin was young, he liked studying plants and animals. Later he studied Latin and Greek at Cambridge University. After university Darwin left Britain on a ship – the *Beagle** – in 1831. His job was to study plants and animals around the world. When he visited the Galapagos islands, Darwin noticed something interesting. There were small (but clear) differences between the same sort of bird living on different islands.

Darwin decided that the birds had changed over time to match their different homes. When an animal was born that fitted better into its home, that animal lived longer and had more children. Animals that didn't fit so well died young. Darwin called his theory 'Evolution'.

Many people in the church didn't like Darwin's ideas. Religion taught that God had made the world in seven days, and that Adam and Eve were the first man and woman. But Darwin said , 'Evolution happens over thousands of years.' He also said, 'People are relatives of the great apes.' These days most people agree with Darwin's theory.

It's strange to think that gorillas are our relatives!

Is it, dear?

Sir Isaac Newton (1642–1727)

Now why did that happen?

At nineteen Newton went to study at Cambridge University. In his second year he went back to his home in the country because of the plague*. One day Newton saw an apple fall from the tree in the garden. He realised that the Earth had something that pulled all things to it. He called this 'something' gravity.

Back at Cambridge, Newton went on to study the stars. He designed a telescope that used mirrors. He was also the first person to realise that white light is made from red, orange, yellow, green, blue and purple light mixed together.

Queen Anne gave Newton the job of looking after the Royal Mint. In 1705 she made him Sir Isaac Newton because of his good work there.

3 **Read the texts again and tick these sentences D (Darwin) or N (Newton).**

		D		N
1 He studied Latin and Greek at Cambridge.		✓	THE	☐
2 He studied Science at Cambridge.		☐	THE	☐
3 He went on a long sea trip.		☐	ORI	☐
4 He travelled on the *Beagle*.		☐	GIN	☐
5 He left Cambridge for a time because of the plague.		☐	PRI	☐
6 He visited the Galapagos Islands.		☐	OFS	☐
7 Differences between birds led to his theory of evolution.		☐	PEC	☐
8 An apple falling from a tree led to his theory of gravity.		☐	NCI	☐
9 He had problems with the church		☐	IES	☐
10 He looked after the Royal Mint.		☐	PIA	☐

4 **What were the names of their great books? Write the letters next to each man's sentences to find their titles.**

1 Darwin's great book was: I H E _ _ _ _ _ _ _ _ _ _ _ _ _ _ _ _ _ _ .

2 Newton's great book was: _ _ _ _ _ _ _ _ _ _ _ _ _ _ . (He wrote it in Latin!)

Personal Project

- Were there any great thinkers in your country's past? When did they live? How did their ideas change the world?
- Find out more about one of them.

*What is it in your language? Find out!

Cars

1 **What do you know about cars? Do the car quiz.**

1 The first cars went at …

  a 30 kilometres an hour.   **b** 8 kilometres an hour.

2 The first cars had …

  a one driver.   **b** two drivers.

3 People first put white lines on the road in …

  a 1925.   **b** 1896.

4 The first traffic jam* happened in …

  a the 1920s.   **b** the 1940s.

5 Today, in British towns, cars can't go faster than …

  a 80 kilometres an hour.   **b** 50 kilometres an hour.

6 In Britain, people drive …

  a on the left.   **b** on the right.

2 **Read the texts and check your answers.**

A short history of cars

In the 19th century*, there weren't many cars. Cars were very slow – they went at 8 kilometres an hour. In 1896, the police gave a man a <u>fine</u> for driving fast. He drove through a town at 14 kilometres an hour. A policeman went after him on his bicycle!

The first cars had two drivers. A third person walked in front with a red flag*. Only rich people had cars. They were open and cold so people in them wore warm clothes. Early cars didn't have <u>indicators</u>. Drivers used their hands for 'left' or 'right'.

By 1904, there were more cars and more <u>speeding</u> fines! In 1925 they put white lines in the <u>middle</u> of the road for the first time. They put <u>traffic lights</u> by the road too. In the same year, the first traffic jam happened in a busy London street. Cars, buses and taxis couldn't move for two hours.

In 1931, traffic <u>accidents</u> were a problem. The British government* said: *Do not read newspapers when you cross the road.* In 1934 the government said to people with big cars: *Do not use your <u>horn</u> after 11.30 at night.* In 1935 the <u>speed limit</u> in British towns was 50 kilometres an hour. It's the same today.

Why do the British drive on the left?

About a quarter of the world drives on the left. Mostly in old British colonies*, like Australia. But why? In the old days, people had swords*. Most people were right-handed. (They usually used their right hands.) So they walked or rode on the left. Then their sword hand was between them and a person coming the opposite way.

In France, it was different. Napoleon was left-handed. So his soldiers* walked on the right. Later, French colonies drove on the right. After 1776 the US and France were friends, so Americans drove on the right. Americans made good cars. People in lots of countries bought them and drove on the right too.

3 Match the underlined words in *A short history of cars* with their meanings.

1 going very fast .... *speeding* ....

2 green, red and yellow lights near the road (A red light means 'Stop'!) ....

3 the centre ....

4 you can hear this part of a car. (Push it when you want to say 'Be careful!') ....

5 lights on a car. They tell other drivers when you are going 'right' or 'left'. ....

6 you must not drive faster than this ....

7 you pay this money to the police when you do something wrong ....

8 when a car hits a person or a different car ....

4 Read about the Mini.
Write the numbers in the correct places.

| 1999 | 5,000 | 70,000 | 147 | ~~1959~~ | four | 40th |

Small but beautiful

The British love the Mini. They made the first one in **1** *1959* .

People wanted a small car for **2** .... people. The Mini's **3** .... 'birthday' was in **4** .... **5** .... Minis and **6** .... people came together for a big party. There are **7** .... different models* of the Mini up to now.

5 Read the texts again and correct the sentences.

1 The first cars drove very ~~quickly~~. *slowly*

2 A person walked behind the car with a flag.

3 The first cars were warm.

4 By the 20th century there were fewer cars.

5 The Australians drive on the right.

6 The British hate the Mini.

Personal Project

- Find out about the history of cars in your country.
- When did people start driving? Do they drive on the right or on the left? What are the speed limits? Is there a favourite car?
- Find out more about one of these things.

* What is it in your language?
Find out!

Trains

Many British people love trains. They don't always travel on them. Some people just like to stand near a railway line and watch them go past! They write down the name, make, and number of each train.

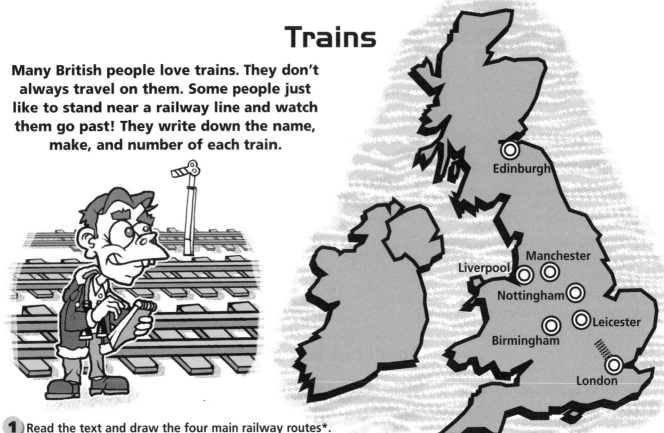

1 Read the text and draw the four main railway routes*.

A brief history of trains

George Stephenson (1781–1848) was the 'father' of British railways. He and his son, Robert (1803–1859), built <u>steam</u> locomotives – <u>engines</u> for pulling trains. From 1830 to 1850 engineers and businessmen built railways all over Britain. The first railway line from Liverpool to Manchester opened in 1830. In 1833 Robert Stephenson became <u>chief engineer</u> on the first railway line from London to Birmingham. They finished it in 1838.

In 1840 people travelled for fun on a train for the first time. It took them from Nottingham to Leicester. They sang all the way! By 1850, there were over 2,500 steam locomotives in Britain. Their highest speed was 125 kilometres an hour. After 1850, Queen Victoria often travelled from London to Edinburgh by train. She went on holiday to Balmoral in Scotland.

Victorian Railway stations were big, high, beautiful buildings. You can see many of them today. In London, there are nine main railway stations. The oldest is London Bridge (1836) and t he newest is Marylebone (1899.) The first electric* railway opened in 1883. It was cleaner and quieter than steam.

In 1914, at the start of World War* I, no town in Britain was more than 32 kilometres from a railway station. Later, cars and aeroplanes became popular, and many smaller railway stations closed. But trains didn't go away. In 1994, the Channel Tunnel* opened. Now people can travel by train under the sea between England and France. It is one of the world's greatest railway <u>projects</u>.

2 Read the text again and put the sentences in order.

a People first travel on a train for fun.

b The first electric railway opens.

c Queen Victoria starts going by train to Scotland for her holidays.

d They build London Bridge Station.

e They build the Channel Tunnel.

f They build Marylebone Station.

g They build the first railway line between Liverpool and Manchester.

h They finish the first railway line from London to Birmingham.

3 Put the letters in the trains in order to make a word. These people watch trains for fun!

T R _ _ _ _ _ _ _ _ _ _ _

4 Match the underlined words in the text with their meanings

1 these make cars or trains move ...._engines_..................

2 the most important ....

3 building plans ....

4 this person builds roads and railways ....

5 this is very hot water when it becomes air ....

5 Complete the text about George Stephenson with the words in the box.

> animals   slowly   son   job   through
> money   built   ~~read~~   hill

George Stephenson couldn't **1** ......_read_.................. until he was 18. When he was 27, he got a **2** .... working with engines. At night, he worked on broken clocks to make more **3** .... In 1814 he **4** .... a steam locomotive. It could pull 30 tons* up a **5** .... at seven kilometres an hour. Before this, people used **6** .... to pull trains. George saw that trains went very **7** .... up hills. He wanted trains to go **8** .... the hills, not over them. He worked with engineers to build flat* railway lines. One of the best engineers was his **9** .... , Robert.

Personal Project

- What do you know about the history of trains in your country?
- Were there any special trains or railway lines? Were there any famous engineers?
- Find out more about one of them.

* What is it in your language? Find out!

Boats

1 Read the texts quickly. Match the people with the boats.

1 Francis Chichester   **a** *Cutty Sark*

2 Admiral Nelson   **b** *B&Q*

3 Brunel   **c** *Gypsy Moth IV*

4 Henry VIII   **d** *Victory*

5 Ellen MacArthur   **e** *Great Eastern*

6 John Willis   **f** *Mary Rose*

Boats in history

Shipbuilding used to be one of Britain's main industries. The famous engineer, Brunel, built some important boats. The *Great Western* (1837) was the first steamship* to travel across the Atlantic. The *Great Eastern* laid the first telegraph cable from Britain to America in 1858.

You can visit some famous British ships today. Here are the top three:
1 The Mary Rose was a 16th century warship. It was King Henry VIII's favourite. It sank in 1545 but was rescued* from the bottom of the sea. Today thousands of people visit it in Portsmouth every year.
2 The Victory is also in Portsmouth. This was Admiral* Nelson's ship in the Battle of Trafalgar in 1805.
3 The Cutty Sark is at Greenwich on the River Thames in London. It was built in Scotland in 1869 for John Willis. It is the last of the 'tea clippers' – boats that transported tea from China to Britain.

The sea is still a challenge* for many British people. In 1967, Sir Francis Chichester arrived in Portsmouth after travelling around the world alone on his yacht*, *Gypsy Moth IV*. It had taken him nine months and he only stopped once, in Sydney, Australia. He was the first man to

sail around the world alone – and he was 65!

In 2001, after 94 days at sea, Ellen MacCarthur became the fastest woman to sail around the world alone. Then, in 2005, aged 28, she became the fastest person – man or woman – to sail alone non-stop around the world. She did it in 71 days in her trimaran, *B&Q*.

2 Read the texts again and correct the sentences.

1 Shipbuilding in Britain used to be less important than it is now.   .... *more* ....

2 Brunel's ships went across the Antarctic Ocean.   ....

3 You can visit the *Mary Rose* and the *Victory* in London.   ....

4 The *Cutty Sark* used to bring tea to Britain from India.   ....

5 In 1967, Francis Chichester went round the world without stopping.   ....

6 Ellen MacArthur was the fastest person to sail round the world alone in 2001.   ....

3 Match the underlined words in the text with their meanings.

1 went down under the sea .... *sank* ....

2 a line that sends electric messages ....

3 a small boat with three main parts ....

4 businesses that make things ....

5 carried or moved ....

6 a big fight ....

4 Complete the text by putting the words in the box into it in the correct places.

line 1: ~~during~~	line 2: trips	line 4: cheaper	line 6: rivers
line 7: restaurants	line 8: sleep	line 10: expensive	line 12: first

Yesterday and today

during

Many canals* were built ᴧ the Industrial Revolution* to transport things. Today, you can make on a canal barge*.

Towards the end of the 20th century, it became to build ships abroad. Many British shipyards* closed. Now many of the old docklands* near the in Britain's cities have houses, offices, and in them.

A popular British holiday is going on a cruise*. You on the boat and stop at different places. The largest and most passenger ship, or liner, in history is the *Queen Mary II* (or *QM2* for short). In January 2005 it celebrated its year of making trips from Britain to the USA.

5 What are these boats? Put the letters in order and find out.

1 LIPCREP .... *clipper* ....

2 CHATY ....

3 ENRIL ....

4 REGAB ....

Personal Project
- Were there any famous boats or captains in your country? What happened to them?
- Did your country have shipping lines in the past? Where did they go and why?
- Find out more about one of these things.

* What is it in your language? Find out!

Marvellous musicians

1 **Match the words with the pictures.**

| comic opera | march | ~~religious~~ | symphony |

1 ....<u>religious</u>...................................

2 ....

3 ....

4 ....

2 **Look at the pictures of the composers Sullivan and Elgar. What do you think they did? Mark these sentences S (Sullivan) or E (Elgar).**

1 He studied* music in Germany.
2 He studied music in an English music shop.
3 He wrote religious music.
4 He wrote symphonies.
5 He wrote marches.
6 He wrote comic operas.

Read the texts and check your ideas.

Gilbert and Sullivan

When Arthur Sullivan (1842–1900) was a boy, he sang for Queen* Victoria. Later, he studied music in England and in Germany. At first he wrote religious music. Queen Victoria loved it. She made him Sir* Arthur Sullivan in 1883.

In 1875 Sullivan met the writer W. S. Gilbert (1836–1911). Together they wrote thirteen comic operas. Gilbert's clever words went very well with Sullivan's music. Two of their most famous operas are *Patience*, and *The Mikado*. (That's the name of an important Japanese man!) *Patience* was about Oscar Wilde and his friends. *The Mikado* was about the Victorian fashion for Japanese things. The operas are very funny. They are still popular* today.

Sir Edward Elgar (1857-1934)

Edward Elgar didn't come from a rich family. His father had a music shop. Edward learnt music there. At first, he wrote music for his friends. But he didn't think it was very good. Then, in 1889, he married* Alice Roberts. She said,

'Your music's beautiful, Edward.' After that, Elgar started to write more. And his music got better.

Enigma *Variations** was Elgar's first great work. He wrote two great symphonies. He also wrote four

fantastic marches and some religious music. When Elgar's wife died in 1920, he was very sad. He wrote very little music in the last 14 years of his life.

Every year, people sing one of Elgar's songs at the Royal Albert Hall in London. It's called *Land* *of Hope and Glory**.

---

3 Correct Mike Mistake's summaries of Sullivan's and Elgar's lives. There are six mistakes in each.

As a boy, Arthur Sullivan sang for Queen ~~Anne~~. Victoria
He studied music in France. The Queen hated his music. Sullivan wrote serious* operas with W.S. Gilbert. One of them – The Mikado – was about the fashion for Chinese things. He became Sir Arthur Sullivan in 1893.

Edward Elgar came from a rich family. His father had a shoe shop. Elgar married in 1998. After that, his music got worse. His last great work was Enigma Variations. He wrote two symphonies and four marches. He wrote a lot of music after his wife died.

Personal Project

- Did your country have any famous composers in the past? When did they live? What kind of music did they write?
- Find out more about one of them.

---

4 Unscramble the words to f**ind the names of three more operas by Gilbert and Sullivan.**

CESSPRIN   ERCROSER   RATSPIE

1 _ _ _ _ _ _ _ _ IDA

2 THE _ _ _ _ _ _ _ _ _

3 THE _ _ _ _ _ _ _
OF PENZANCE

* What is it in your language? Find out!

Clever craftsmen*

1 Look at the pictures and read the definitions. What are the jobs?

1 This person makes pots.

p o t t e r

2 This person plans buildings.

_ r c _ t _ _ _

3 This person designs things for a house. _ _ _ _ _ g n _ _

4 This person asks for votes*.

p _ l _ _ c _ _ _

5 This person makes beautiful things

c r _ _ w _ k _ _

6 This person paints pictures.

_ a _ n _ _ _

7 This man makes money in business.

_ u _ _ n _ _ m _ _

8 This person publishes books.

p _ _ l _ _ h _ _

9 This person writes poems.

_ o _ _

Josiah Wedgwood (1730–1795)

Josiah Wedgwood's family had a pottery factory* in Staffordshire in the north of England. When he was nine, he started to work as a potter there. He was brilliant. In 1759 Josiah started his own pottery factory. It made some beautiful plates, teacups and teapots for the wife of King George III. Soon, everyone in England wanted Wedgwood pottery. Josiah was not just a good craftsman, he was a good businessman!

The most famous Wedgwood pottery is blue with white Greek or Roman figures* on it. Josiah took the idea from old Greek and Roman pottery. You can still buy this Wedgwood pottery in Britain today.

2 **Read the texts about Josiah Wedgwood and William Morris. Which jobs from activity 1 did each man do?**

1 Josiah Wedgwood: .... , ... , ...

2 William Morris: .... , ... , ... , ... ,

.... , ... , ...

William Morris (1834–1896)

William Morris studied at Oxford University*. After university, he worked for a short time as an architect, but he was bored. After that, he became a painter, then a designer. He started a company* with a group of craftworkers to make beautiful furniture. Many of William Morris's designs have animals, birds, plants, and flowers in them. In his free time he wrote poems and stories. Lots of his poems were about Iceland.

Then Morris became a politician. He wanted to help poor working people. He spoke at political meetings all over Britain. Morris got into trouble with the police because of his politics.

In 1891 Morris started publishing fine books with lovely covers* and beautiful pictures inside. He called his publishing company the Kelmscott Press*.

3 **Read the texts again. Mark these sentences W (Wedgwood) or M (Morris).**

	W	M
1 His family had a factory.	☑ CH	☐
2 He studied at Oxford University.	☐	WA ☐
3 He started work when he was nine.	☐ AR	☐
4 He had his own factory when he was 29.	☐	LO ☐
5 Plants and animals are in many of his designs.	☐ LL	☐
6 He became a politician.	☐	PA ☐
7 He made blue and white pottery.	☐ TT	☐
8 He wanted to help poor people.	☐	PE ☐
9 He made things for George III's wife.	☐ E	☐
10 He wrote poems about Iceland.	☐	R ☐

4 **Put the letters next to the boxes you ticked for each man in order. Find these words:**

1 Wedgwood made pottery for this Queen. _ _ _ _ _ _ _ _ _ _ _

2 Morris's most famous designs are on this. _ _ _ _ _ _ _ _ _ _

5 **Play 'Guess the Job'.**
Choose a job from activity 1. Write it down but don't tell your partner. She/he must guess the job by asking questions, for example: 'Do you use your hands?'

Rules
- You have only five questions.
- You can't ask questions like 'Are you a potter?'
- You can't use mime*.
- You can answer only 'yes' or 'no.'

Personal Project
- Were there any famous artists or craftworkers in your country? Where did they live and work? What did they do?
- Find out more about one of them.

* What is it in your language? Find out!

Joseph Paxton and the Crystal Palace

1 Match the words in the water lily with these definitions. Complete the puzzle.

1 to put money into a business
2 this metal is very strong and cheap
3 the ruler of a small country (or the son of a king or queen)
4 a place that has many interesting things on show
5 a copy that someone makes of something real
6 lots of lands around the world that belong to one country
7 these very big animals lived on earth before people
8 a clear inexpensive stone with no colour

words in the water lily: crystal, dinosaur, iron, prince, empire, exhibition, invest, model

1 i n v e s t

2

3

4

5

6

7

8

2 Paxton grew a water lily from Guiana in the glasshouse at Chatsworth. What name did he give to the flower? Look at the black squares in the puzzle to find it.

V _ _ _ _ _ _ _

3 Look at the two texts and answer these questions.

1 What was the Crystal Palace?

a an exhibition building   **b** a palace for Queen Victoria

2 What was the Crystal Palace made of?

a crystal   **b** iron and glass

3 What was the connection between Paxton and the Crystal Palace?

a he paid for it   **b** he was the architect

4 Read the texts again and correct these false sentences.

1 Paxton worked as a ~~pilot~~ *gardener* for The Duke of Devonshire.

2 He invested a lot of money in airports.

3 He became a poor man.

4 He started a magazine.

5 Prince Edward, Victoria's son, organised the Great Exhibition.

6 They built the Science Museum with money from the Great Exhibition.

7 Paxton opened the Crystal Palace again in North London.

8 A big fire destroyed the Crystal Palace in 1963.

Sir Joseph Paxton (1801–65)

Paxton worked as a gardener for the Duke* of Devonshire. He also taught himself to be an architect and designed buildings. One of these was a glasshouse for the gardens at Chatsworth, the Duke's country house. He copied the design of the water lily leaves to make his glasshouse light but strong. Paxton was also interested in railways. He invested a lot of money in them and became a rich man. With his money he started a newspaper – the Daily News – with Charles Dickens as the editor*.

The Crystal Palace

In 1851 Prince Albert, Queen Victoria's husband, organised* a Great Exhibition in Hyde Park in London. He wanted to show British people things from the different countries in the British Empire. Paxton designed the huge glass and iron building for the exhibition. People loved it and called it the Crystal Palace. Paxton became Sir Joseph Paxton in 1851. The Great Exhibition was a success. The money from it helped to build the Victoria and Albert Museum in Kensington. You can still visit it today.

When the Great Exhibition closed in 1852, Paxton moved the Crystal Palace to South London. It opened again in 1854 as one of the first theme parks in the world. There were different halls inside the building – Roman, Greek, Egyptian, and Italian. In the park outside there were life-size models of dinosaurs. It was a fantastic day out for Victorian families.

A big fire destroyed the Crystal Palace in 1936. But that part of London is still called Crystal Palace. And you can still see the model dinosaurs in the park.

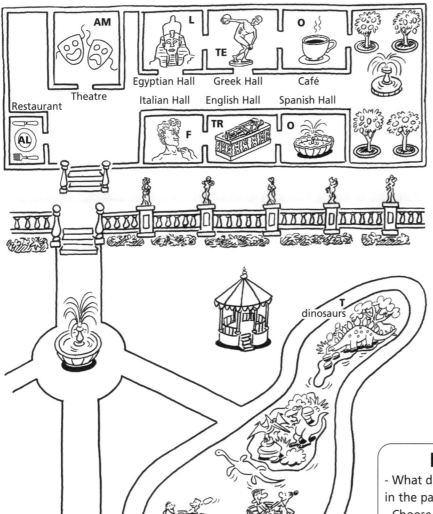

5 **Read a Victorian boy's diary about a day at the Palace. Draw his route on the map above.**

15th July 1865
Today we visited the Crystal Palace. First we visited the Italian Hall and the Spanish Hall. Then we went to the café for a drink. After that we went out into the park. We saw the dinosaurs, and we took a boat out on the lake. Then we went back to the restaurant for lunch. In the afternoon we visited the Egyptian Hall and the Greek Hall. Then we went to see a show in the theatre in the evening. It was a great day out!

6 **'Crystal Palace' is also the name of something else. Write the capital letters on the map in order to find it.**

A _ _ _ _ _ _ _ _

_ _ _ _

Personal Project

- What did people do for fun in your country in the past?
- Choose one time in your country's history. Find out about leisure activities for people in those days.

* What is it in your language? Find out!

North America

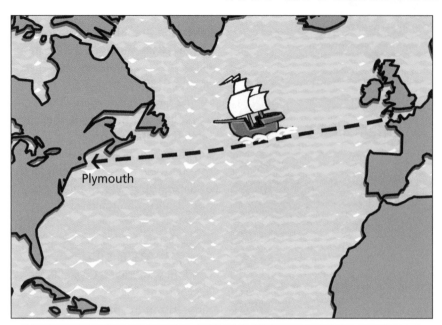

Plymouth

The British in America

In 1600 some ships went from Britain to North America. There, the British found new places and useful things. They brought <u>tobacco</u> and <u>potatoes</u> from America, and <u>furs</u> from Canada.

One of Britain's first colonies* was Virginia. Sir* Walter Raleigh named it after <u>Queen</u> Elizabeth I, the 'Virgin* Queen.'

In 1620, 102 English people arrived in America on their boat, the *Mayflower*. They were the Pilgrim* Fathers. They built houses and started a new town, Plymouth. Native Americans – the people already living there – spoke different languages. But the British wanted to speak English. Later, there were English colonies all along the Atlantic coast* of America.

People from other countries also went to America. Britain and France fought* with each other over the land*. The British got more land, but they didn't have it for long. Britain lost thirteen

colonies during the Revolution* (1775-1781). That was the start of the United States of America.

In the 1790s and 1800s some more British people decided to go and live in North America and 'New England' got its name. Many of the people were English <u>farmers</u> and <u>factory</u> workers without jobs. A lot of Scottish people went to Canada at this time. They called the land on the east coast of Canada 'Nova Scotia'. (That means 'New Scotland'.)

In 1830 a man from the north of England went to America to find a new life. He wrote a letter to his wife in 1831. She was still in England at the time. This is part of it.

Dear Wife,
I am much heavier* than when I arrived. Life is good here. When I sit down to eat, I always think of the hungry workers back in England.

---

1 Match the underlined words in the text with the pictures.

1 .... furs ....

2 ....

3 ....

4 ....

5 ....

6 ....

2 Read the text again. Mark these sentences True or False.

1 Virginia gets its name from Elizabeth I, the Virgin Queen. ....True.........

2 The Pilgrim Fathers went to live in an old Native American town. ....

3 People from different countries went to America after the Pilgrim Fathers. ....

4 Britain lost 13 colonies in North America in the 1790s. ....

5 Many people left Britain because they were hungry and had no work. ....

6 Parts of North America have British place names. ....

3 Complete the sentences with *someone*, *anyone*, *everyone*, or *no one*.

Thanksgiving

1 When the Pilgrim Fathers arrived in America, there wasn't ....anyone.......... to meet them.

2 The next autumn*, ... said, 'Let's cook a special dinner with the fruit and vegetables from our farms!'

3 .... said 'yes' – because they all wanted to have some fun.

4 At first, ... wanted to ask the Native Americans, because they were frightened of them.

5 Then .... said, 'We must ask them. This is their country, too.'

6 The dinner was very good, and .... had a good time.

This dinner was the first Thanksgiving. The Pilgrim Fathers said 'thank you' for all their food. Thanksgiving Day is still a special day in America. On the fourth Thursday in November, each family in the USA meets for a special dinner.

4 Find the names in the word square and complete the sentences.

1 The first British colony in America was ....Virginia........... .

2 The ....
went to America in 1620.

3 The name of their boat was The ....

4 They built a town and called it ....

5 A lot of people went from .... to Canada.

M	T	E	A	O	A	Z	Y	N	A	T	S	L	A
P	I	L	G	R	I	M	F	A	T	H	E	R	S
L	N	S	F	X	H	A	S	T	D	S	O	E	C
Y	Y	E	E	W	E	Y	D	A	G	E	E	X	O
M	S	T	E	K	D	F	R	T	N	H	Y	S	T
O	A	S	L	D	A	L	A	Y	S	A	G	H	L
U	E	R	T	F	R	O	M	T	E	W	M	O	A
T	Y	T	M	P	D	W	T	D	L	E	D	D	N
H	Y	S	S	Y	N	E	N	W	E	E	D	A	D
O	A	Y	D	V	I	R	G	I	N	I	A	T	E

Personal Project

- Did any people from your country go across the sea to live in a different country? When did they go? Where did they go? What happened to them?
- Find out more about some of them.

*What is it in your language? Find out!

Australia and New Zealand

1 Match the headings with the different parts of the text.

1 Independence*
2 The first colony
3 ~~Captain* Cook~~
4 Australia today
5 The convicts arrive
6 World Wars
7 Things get better

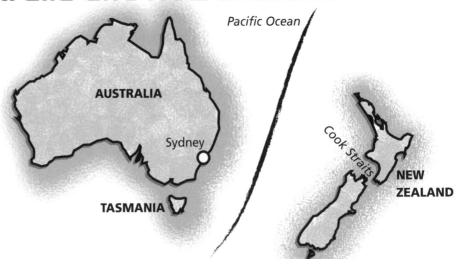

Pacific Ocean

AUSTRALIA

Sydney

Cook Straits

TASMANIA

NEW ZEALAND

Australia

a .... Captain Cook ....

In 1768 Britain sent Captain James Cook to search for the Unknown South Land. In 1770 he reached the east coast of Australia. He called this area New South Wales.

b ....

The British government* sent eleven boats to Australia in 1788. They were full of convicts – people from prisons. It took boats many weeks to travel to Australia. Life on the convict ships was horrible. The convicts couldn't move, and a lot of them became ill or died. The worst convicts went to Tasmania.

c ....

The first British colony in Australia was in Sydney. At first, there were a lot of problems. The Aborigines – the people already living there – were unfriendly. Some of the convicts didn't want to work. Many of them were there for small crimes*, and they felt that this was unfair. Times were hard, and there wasn't enough food.

d ....

After 1810 things began to change. More people arrived from Britain. They were not convicts. They really wanted to be in Australia. It was a big country, and the land was good. These people started farms

with sheep* and cattle*. Some of the convicts became free, and they stayed in Australia to work. Slowly, things got better, and people made more money. In 1851 someone found gold* in New South Wales. Suddenly, a lot more people wanted to go to Australia! Britain finally stopped sending convicts to Australia in 1853.

e ....

Between 1859 and 1890, the different British colonies in Australia became a bit more independent*. Everyone could vote* except the Aborigines. (They got the vote in 1966.) In 1901, the different colonies came together. Australia became one country then – with its own government.

f ....

Australia still felt British in some ways. Thousands of Australian soldiers* died when Australia helped Britain in World Wars* I and II.

g ....

Now, Australia and Britain are friends. British people still go to Australia to find a better life. They feel at home there because most people speak English. But in the last 50 years, people have moved to Australia from all over the world. In Australian cities today, you can hear many different languages – not just English.

2 Read the text again. Choose the best words to complete these sentences.

1 The first British people to arrive in Australia from Britain were convicts / Aborigines.

2 Compared to Britain, Australia is very big / small.

3 People went to Australia to build schools / farms.

4 People hoped to become rich / poor in Australia.

5 Australia became one country in 1859 / in 1901

6 Australians fought with / against Britain in the two World Wars.

3 Read this page from the diary of a young convict in Sydney. Some of the words are incomplete. Can you complete them?

At last we've arrived in this 1 <u>un</u>known land. On the boat there were six of us in one small room. One of them was a killer. The others were just 2 ......lucky. They used false money, or couldn't pay money back to someone. I took some bread from a shop! It's very 3 ......fair. My friend John died on the boat. He became ill, and it was 4 ......possible to help him. Here in Australia we work very hard. It's hot, and our clothes are 5 ......comfortable. The Aborigines are 6 ......friendly, but I can understand that. They were here first, and now 7 ......kind white men are taking their land from them. This morning, my friend Sam 8 ......appeared. He's escaped, but they'll catch him. Then he'll go to Tasmania, and I'll never see him again. I'm so 9 ......happy.
They say that Australia is an 10 ......usual land, full of strange trees and animals. But I'm not free to see it. Sometimes my life as a convict seems 11 ......real. Then I dream that I'm a free man again with my own farm. Will it happen one day? I hope so!

4 Match the sentence halves, and find out about New Zealand.

New Zealand

1 Captain Cook went round the

2 The first European born in New Zealand

3 The Maori people lived in New Zealand

4 New Zealand became

5 By 1859, there were more

6 New Zealand was the first country

7 Until the 1970s, New Zealand sent

8 There are more sheep

9 New Zealand has a lot of

10 New Zealand is the place in

a before the Europeans arrived. L

b than people in New Zealand. T

c New Zealand coast between 1769 and 1770. W

d the popular film, The Lord* of the Rings*. N

e beautiful mountains and rivers. O

f a British colony in 1840. L

g was Thomas King (in 1815). E

h a lot of meat and butter to Britain. G

i Europeans than Maori people in New Zealand. I

j to give women the vote (in 1893). N

Did you know?

Kangaroos are all over Australia, but there aren't any in New Zealand. They are a problem because they jump out in front of cars. Farmers don't like them because they take their animals' food!

5 Put the letters in the sheep in order to find the capital of New Zealand.

<u>W</u> _ _ _ _ _ _ _ _ _

Personal Project

- Are there people from other countries living in your country?
- When did they come? Why did they come?
- Find out more about some of them.

*What is it in your language? Find out!

India

1 **What do you know about India? Do the India quiz.**

1 Which drink comes from India?

   a beer   **b** tea

2 Who were the leaders in India before the British?

   a the princes   **b** the farmers

3 Who was the British Queen when Britain was strong in India?

   a Elizabeth II   **b** Victoria

4 Who wanted independence for India?

   a Gandhi   **b** Victoria

5 When did India become an independent country?

   a 1847   **b** 1947

6 Which of these sports did Britain take to India?

   a basketball   **b** cricket

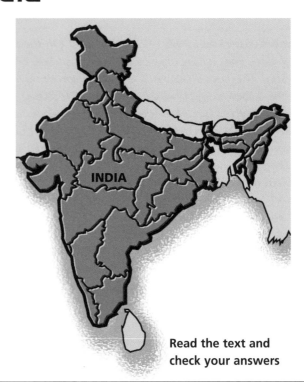

Read the text and check your answers

The British in India

Lots of European countries were interested in India and the Far East. There were useful and beautiful things there, like silk, spices – and tea!

The British East India Company ruled* India for many years. It was set up in 1600, when lots of different princes ruled different parts of the country. The Company bought and sold things, and became very strong. Not everyone was happy with this. In 1857 many Indians fought against the British. Many died. The British won, because their army was stronger. Also, many Indian soldiers fought on the British side. But it was the end of the Company's rule. From 1858, the British Crown ruled India. Queen Victoria became Empress* of India in 1877.

Later, more and more Indians wanted independence for their country. The most famous of these was Mahatma Gandhi, the 'father' of modern India. He and his followers worked for independence. They believed in non-violent action like hunger strikes.

India became independent in 1947. It was divided* into two countries, India and Pakistan. In 1950, India became a republic but it stayed in the Commonwealth. (This is a group of countries that Britain has ruled.)

Britain took these things to India: the game of cricket, railways, laws, the English language, and Christianity*. In the 1950s and 1960s, a lot of people from India came to live in Britain. They brought their own customs* and languages with them. Asian food, films, and music are all popular in Britain now.

2 Match the underlined words in the text with their meanings.

1 when you stop eating because you don't agree with something .... *hunger strikes* ....

2 you can add these to food to give it a good taste ....

3 a country without a king or queen ....

4 peaceful, without fighting ....

5 the ruling king or queen (also the 'hat' worn by the king or queen) ....

6 clothes made of this are soft and nice to touch ....

3 Read the text again and put these sentences in order.

a People come from India to live in Britain.

b India and Pakistan become independent.

c The British Crown takes over India.

d The East India Company is started.

e Ghandi works for Indian independence.

f India becomes a republic.

g Many Indians fight against the British.

h Asian things become popular in Britain.

i Queen Victoria becomes Empress of India.

4 Put the letters in the teacups in order to find the name of the Indian film industry.
(India makes more films than any other country in the world!)

— — — — — — — — —

5 Some Indian words have entered the English language. Do you know what they are?
Unjumble the letters and find out.

1 RUCYR

2 JASPMAY

3 NUBLAGWO

This meal is made with meat and vegetables in a spicy sauce* with rice.

You wear these in bed

This is a house with no upstairs

— — — — — — — — — — — — — — — — — — —

Did you know?

From 1858 the British government sent 'Viceroys' to India. They ruled the country for the King or Queen of Britain. The last of the British Viceroys was Lord* Mountbatten. He was the uncle of Prince Charles, son of Queen Elizabeth II. Lord Mountbatten was killed by the IRA (Irish Republican Army) in 1979.

Personal Project

- Think of some things in your country that come from another country (words, food, music, clothes, games, films, etc). Where are they from?
- Find out when these things were introduced into your country.

*What is it in your language? Find out!

Quiz 1

Choose the best answer for each question.

A The United Kingdom – Wales against the world

1 What is the capital of Wales?
a Dublin ❑   **b** London ❑   **c** Cardiff ❑

2 What can you see on the Welsh flag?
a a fish ❑   **b** a dragon ❑   **c** a dog ❑

3 What do we call the son of a king and queen?
a a prince ❑   **b** a princess ❑   **c** a soldier ❑

B Kings and queens – Crazy Kings

1 How many wives did Henry VIII have?
a seven ❑   **b** four ❑   **c** six ❑

2 What did the British call George III?
a 'the Farmer King' ❑   **b** 'the German King' ❑   **c** 'the Book-loving King' ❑

3 What happened to George III?
a His son killed him. ❑   **b** He talked to trees. ❑   **c** He killed his wife. ❑

C Historic buildings – The Queen's homes

1 What is the name of Queen Elizabeth II's house in Scotland?
a Balmoral ❑   **b** Windsor ❑   **c** Buckingham ❑

2 What happened at Windsor Castle in the early 1990s?
a a garden party ❑   **b** a fire ❑   **c** a football game ❑

3 What can you see every day outside Buckingham Palace?
a the Changing of the Guard ❑   **b** the Queen on her horse ❑   **c** a pop concert ❑

D Famous explorers – Sea explorers

1 When did Sir Francis Drake live?
a the 12th century ❑   **b** the 16th century ❑   **c** the 19th century ❑

2 What did Sir Walter Raleigh look for in South America?
a lost British people ❑   **b** new boats ❑   **c** El Dorado ❑

3 What did Raleigh bring back to Britain?
a coconuts ❑   **b** potatoes and tobacco ❑   **c** his parents ❑

E Famous women – Florence Nightingale

1 Florence Nightingale is often called 'The Lady with the ...'
a light ❑   **b** lamp ❑   **c** love ❑

2 Florence is famous for her work in ....
a schools ❑   **b** restaurants ❑   **c** hospitals ❑

3 Which country did she work in during the Crimean War?
a Italy ❑   **b** Russia ❑   **c** Turkey ❑

F Famous men – They cared for poor workers

1 What did William Wilberforce fight against?
a the slave trade ❑   **b** working women ❑   **c** Africans ❑

2 What did Wilberforce become when he was only 21?
a Prime Minister ❑   **b** Doctor Wilberforce ❑   **c** a Member of Parliament ❑

3 What did George Cadbury make in his factory?
a clothes ❑   **b** chocolate ❑   **c** shoes ❑

G Dreadful disasters – The great fire of London

1 When was the Great Fire of London?
a 1466 ❑   **b** 1666 ❑   **c** 1866 ❑

2 Which building burned down in the fire?
a Saint Paul's Hospital ❑   **b** Saint Paul's School ❑   **c** St Paul's Cathedral ❑

3 How did most people escape from the fire?
a They used horses. ❑   **b** They went on boats down the river. ❑   **c** They went into churches. ❑

H The worst wars –
The wars of the roses

1 Which two families fought in the Wars of the Roses?
a Nottingham and   **b** Tudor and   **c** York and
Manchester ❑   Bosworth ❑   Lancaster ❑

2 Which kind of wife did Warwick want for
    Edward IV?
a a German   **b** a French   **c** an English
wife ❑   wife ❑   wife ❑

3 What happened to the two young princes in
    the Tower?
a They died. ❑   **b** They killed   **c** They became
                       their uncle. ❑   kings of
                                          England. ❑

I Wonderful writers –
Three great writers

1 Which is the correct name of the book by
    Geoffrey Chaucer?
a The Canterbury   **b** The Canterbury   **c** The Canterbury
Pilgrims ❑   Stories ❑   Tales ❑

2 Which is the correct name of the play by
    William Shakespeare?
a Hamlet and   **b** Juliet and   **c** Romeo and
Romeo ❑   Hamlet ❑   Juliet ❑

3 What is Oliver Twist?
a a play by   **b** a novel by   **c** a poem
Shakespeare ❑   Charles Dickens ❑   by Geoffrey
                                               Chaucer ❑

J Inventions, discoveries and science –
They changed their world

1 Who started the first printing press in Britain?
a Geoffrey   **b** Gutenberg ❑   **c** William
Chaucer ❑   Caxton ❑

2 Who did the British call 'the father of television'?
a Charles   **b** John Logie   **c** Alexander
Babbage ❑   Baird ❑   Graham Bell ❑

3 Who did <u>not</u> work with computers?
a Ada Lovelace ❑   **b** Alexander   **c** Charles
                          Graham Bell ❑   Babbage ❑

K Transport – Cars

1 Which of these is part of a car?
a traffic lights ❑   **b** traffic jam ❑   **c** indicators ❑

2 In which country do people drive on the right?
a the USA ❑   **b** Britain ❑   **c** Australia ❑

4 Which small car do people like a lot in Britain?
a the Maxi ❑   **b** the Minor ❑   **c** the Mini ❑

L Music, art, crafts and leisure –
Marvellous musicians

1 What did Gilbert and Sullivan write together?
a symphonies ❑   **b** comic operas ❑   **c** religious
                                             music ❑

2 Who made Arthur Sullivan a 'Sir'?
a Edward VII ❑   **b** William IV ❑   **c** Queen
                                          Victoria ❑

3 What kind of music did Edward Elgar write?
a guitar music ❑   **b** symphonies   **c** film music ❑
                          and marches ❑

M Britain and the world –
North America

1 What was the name of one of Britain's first colonies
    in North America?
a Queensland ❑   **b** Virginia ❑   **c** Elizabeth ❑

2 What were the first British colonists in North
    America called?
a the   **b** the Natives ❑   **c** the Pilgrim
Mayflowers ❑   Fathers ❑

3 Why did a lot of British people go to North America
    in the 1800s?
a They liked the   **b** They couldn't   **c** They liked the
food there. ❑   find work in   weather better
                       Britain. ❑   in America. ❑

Score: .... **out of 39 points.**

Quiz 2

Choose the best answer for each question.

A The United Kingdom –
Scotland for ever!

1 **What did people call the Scottish fighter William Wallace?**

a Bravehand ❑   **b** Bigfoot ❑   **c** Braveheart ❑

2 **What were Elizabeth I and Mary Queen of Scots?**

a sisters ❑   **b** cousins ❑   **c** friends ❑

3 **What happened to Mary Queen of Scots?**

a She died ❑ in France.   **b** She became ❑ Queen of England.   **c** Elizabeth I ❑ executed her.

B Kings and queens – Cool queens

1 **Which queen was the 'Virgin Queen'?**

a Elizabeth I ❑   **b** Mary Queen of Scots ❑   **c** Victoria ❑

2 **Who was a famous writer when Elizabeth I was queen?**

a William Blake ❑   **b** Oscar Wilde ❑   **c** William Shakespeare ❑

3 **Where was Victoria's husband, Albert, from?**

a France ❑   **b** Scotland ❑   **c** Germany ❑

C Historic buildings – A prison and a palace

1 **What <u>didn't</u> they use the Tower of London for in the past?**

a a prison ❑   **b** a restaurant ❑   **c** a zoo ❑

2 **What is the name of the guards at the Tower of London?**

a Meateaters ❑   **b** Londoners ❑   **c** Beefeaters ❑

3 **Which king lived at Hampton Court Palace?**

a James I ❑   **b** Henry VIII ❑   **c** William I ❑

D Famous explorers – Extreme explorers

1 **Who was the first man to reach the South Pole?**

a Sir Ernest Shackleton ❑   **b** Captain Scott ❑   **c** Roald Amundsen ❑

2 **What happened to Captain Scott and his men?**

a They died in the Antarctic. ❑   **b** They died in the First World War. ❑   **c** They returned to Britain. ❑

3 **What happened to Sir Ernest Shackleton's boat, the *Endurance*?**

a There was a fire on it. ❑   **b** The ice broke it. ❑   **c** Animals attacked it. ❑

E Famous women – Elizabeth Fry

1 **Elizabeth Fry is famous for her work with** …

a prisoners ❑   **b** teachers ❑   **c** writers ❑

2 **Elizabeth Fry's husband was…**

a a prisoner ❑   **b** a London merchant ❑   **c** a prison guard ❑

3 **Elizabeth Fry was against** …

a big families ❑   **b** rich people ❑   **c** hanging ❑

F Famous men –
They helped young people

1 **What did Lord Baden Powell start?**

a the town of Mafeking ❑   **b** the Boy Scouts ❑   **c** the Boer War ❑

2 **Where did Baden Powell go when he was in the army?**

a South Africa ❑   **b** South America ❑   **c** Canada ❑

3 **What did Lord Shaftesbury help to stop?**

a children going to school ❑   **b** children going to hospital ❑   **c** children going out to work ❑

G Dreadful disasters – The Black Death

1 When did the Black Death first come to Britain?
a the 10th century b the 12th century c the 14th
❑   ❑   century ❑

2 What was the cause of the Black Death?
a bad water ❑   b germs on rats ❑   c eating cats
                                       and dogs ❑

3 When a family got the plague, what did people draw on their front door?
a a face ❑   b a cross ❑   c a star ❑

H The worst wars – The English civil war

1 In the English Civil War, who followed Charles I?
a the Roundheads b the Cavaliers ❑   c the Scots ❑
❑

2 Who followed Oliver Cromwell?
a the Scottish   b the Cavaliers   c the
Church ❑   ❑   Roundheads ❑

3 What happened to Charles I?
a He ran away   b He married an   c They cut off
to Holland. ❑   orange-seller. ❑   his head. ❑

I Wonderful writers – Women writers

1 In Jane Austen's novels, the women usually want to find ...
a a house ❑   b a car ❑   c a husband ❑

2 George Eliot was more interested in .... than Jane Austen.
a people ❑   b politics ❑   c writing ❑

3 All the Bronte sisters died ...
a young ❑   b unmarried ❑   c rich ❑

J Inventions, discoveries and science – They discovered it

1 What did Edward Jenner call his discovery?
a vaccination ❑   b injection ❑   c liquid ❑

2 What happened as a result of Joseph Lister's work?
a Doctors wore   b More people   c Fewer people
ordinary clothes died after   died after
when they did   operations. ❑   operations. ❑
operations. ❑

3 What did Alexander Fleming discover?
a germs ❑   b penicillin ❑   c mould ❑

K Transport – Trains

1 What do we call a person who watches trains for fun?
a a trainfollower b a locomotive   c a trainspotter
❑   ❑   ❑

2 What did George and Robert Stephenson do?
a They took   b They built   c They built
Queen Victoria   railway stations   engines for
to Scotland. ❑   in London. ❑   pulling trains. ❑

3 Which two countries does the Channel Tunnel join?
a Ireland and   b England and   c England and
England ❑   France ❑   Holland ❑

L Music, arts, crafts and leisure – Clever craftsmen

1 What did Josiah Wedgwood make?
a postcards and   b cups and plates   c tables and
posters ❑   ❑   chairs ❑

2 What colour is the most famous Wedgwood pottery?
a red and white   b yellow and   c light blue
❑   orange ❑   and white ❑

3 What did William Morris design?
a ships ❑   b furniture ❑   c shoes ❑

M Britain and the world – Australia and New Zealand

1 Who discovered Australia for the British?
a Captain Scott   b Charles Darwin   c Captain Cook
❑   ❑   ❑

2 Who did the British government first send to Australia?
a doctors   b convicts   c teachers

3 Who are the native people of New Zealand?
a the Maori people b the Aborigines   c the British
❑   ❑   ❑

Score: .... **out of 39 points.**

Quiz 3

Choose the best answer for each question.

A The United Kingdom – The Irish question

1 Who is the patron saint of Ireland?
a Saint Andrew ❏   b Saint George ❏   c Saint Patrick ❏

2 What are the two main religious groups in Ireland?
a Catholic and Roman ❏   b Protestant and Christian ❏   c Catholic and Protestant ❏

3 What is the IRA?
a Irish Red Army ❏   b Irish Republican Army ❏   c Irish Rescue Army ❏

B Kings and queens – Romantic royals

1 Why did Edward VIII give up the throne?
a to go and live abroad ❏   b to marry a divorced woman ❏   c to go and work for the Church ❏

2 What happened to Lady Diana Spencer?
a She married an American. ❏   b She went to live in India. ❏   c She died in a car crash. ❏

3 What are the names of Charles's two sons?
a Warren and James ❏   b Tony and Harris ❏   c William and Harry ❏

C Historic buildings – Top universities: Oxford and Cambridge

1 Where did English students study before they went to Oxford or Cambridge?
a London University ❏   b the Sorbonne, Paris ❏   c Edinburgh University ❏

2 What couldn't the teachers at Oxford and Cambridge do before the 19th century?
a smoke ❏   b play tennis ❏   c marry ❏

3 What do Oxford and Cambridge have every year?
a a big dinner ❏   b a fashion show ❏   c a boat race ❏

D Famous explorers – Explorers in Africa

1 Which of these people was not an explorer in Africa?
a Richard Burton ❏   b Mungo Park ❏   c Francis Drake ❏

2 What did early explorers in Africa want to find?
a the mouth of the Nile ❏   b the source of the Nile ❏   c the smallest lake ❏

3 What was the job of the explorer David Livingstone?
a writer ❏   b reporter ❏   c doctor ❏

E Famous women – Votes for women

1 What did the suffragettes want for women?
a more food ❏   b the vote ❏   c more money ❏

2 Who was Emmeline Pankhurst?
a a Member of Parliament ❏   b the first woman Prime Minister ❏   c a suffragette leader ❏

3 What happened during the First World War?
a women became politicians ❏   b women did men's jobs ❏   c women went to fight ❏

F Famous men – Famous fighters

1 What did Admiral Nelson lose in battle?
a his leg ❏   b an eye and an arm ❏   c an ear ❏

2 Who did he fight at the Battle of Trafalgar?
a the French and Spanish ❏   b the Spanish and Italians ❏   c the Portuguese and Germans ❏

3 Who did the Duke of Wellington fight against?
a the Belgians ❏   b Napoleon ❏   c the Portuguese ❏

G Dreadful disasters – The *Titanic*

1 Where was the *Titanic* going when the accident happened?
a to England ❏   b to Ireland ❏   c to New York ❏

2 What did the *Titanic* hit?
a another boat ❏   b an iceberg ❏   c a rock ❏

3 What did most people say about the *Titanic* before the accident?

a 'It will never sink.' ❑
b 'It's too big to float.' ❑
c 'It will travel very slowly.' ❑

H The worst wars – Two world wars

1 Who was shot just before World War I?

a Benito Mussolini ❑
b Wilhelm II ❑
c Franz Ferdinand of Austria ❑

2 Where did most of the British army go to fight during World War I?

a Germany ❑
b France ❑
c Japan ❑

3 Who was the Prime Minister of Britain during World War II?

a Joseph Stalin ❑
b Wilhelm II ❑
c Winston Churchill ❑

I Wonderful writers – Romantic poets

1 What was happening in the world at the time of the Romantic poets?

a bad weather ❑
b revolutions ❑
c the start of cinema ❑

2 Which poet wrote about an old sailor lost at sea?

a Coleridge ❑
b Shelley ❑
c Blake ❑

3 Which of these words describes someone who is 'Byronic'?

a bored ❑
b scary ❑
c a rebel ❑

J Inventions, discoveries and science – Great thinkers

1 Why is Sir Isaac Newton famous?

a because he explained gravity ❑
b because he spoke lots of languages ❑
c because he discovered new stars ❑

2 What did Newton design?

a a mirror ❑
b a garden ❑
c a telescope ❑

3 Why is Charles Darwin famous?

a for his love of animals ❑
b for his theory of evolution ❑
c for his drawings of plants ❑

K Transport – Boats

1 What was Isambard Kingdom Brunel's job?

a He was a sailor. ❑
b He was an engineer. ❑
c He was a painter. ❑

2 What was the name of Admiral Nelson's ship at the battle of Trafalgar?

a the *Cutty Sark* ❑
b the *Mary Rose* ❑
c the *Victory* ❑

3 What did Ellen MacArthur do?

a She sailed around the world alone. ❑
b She built a trimaran. ❑
c She went to Australia in a yacht. ❑

L Music, arts, craft and leisure – Joseph Paxton and the Crystal Palace

1 What did Joseph Paxton build?

a the Royal Albert Hall ❑
b the Crystal Palace ❑
c Buckingham Palace ❑

2 Who organised the Great Exhibition in 1851 in London?

a the Egyptians ❑
b Prince Albert ❑
c Queen Victoria ❑

3 What could you see at the Great Exhibition?

a real dinosaurs ❑
b kings and queens ❑
c things from different countries ❑

M Britain and the world – India

1 Which of these things did Britain take from India?

a silk and spices ❑
b cricket ❑
c railways ❑

2 Who became 'Empress of India' in 1877 ?

a Queen Elizabeth ❑
b Lady Mountbatten ❑
c Queen Victoria ❑

3 Which of these did Mahatma Gandhi use to get independence for India?

a attacks on churches
b hunger strikes
c fighting with British soldiers

Score: .... **out of 39 points.**

GORILLA

Answers

THE UNITED KINGDOM

pages 6–7
* WALES AGAINST THE WORLD

1 Wales is on the left and England on the right.

2 1 LONDON 2 CARDIFF

4 2 king 3 queen 4 prince 5 princess

5 a 5 b 4 c 3 d 1 e 2 f 7 g 6

6 Possible Answer: First the Celts came to live in Wales. Then the Romans arrived in Wales. Next, the Anglo Saxons arrived in England. After that, an English king made his son the first English Prince of Wales. Next, there was the first Welsh king of England. In the end, Henry VIII made Wales part of England.

pages 8–9
** SCOTLAND FOR EVER!
1

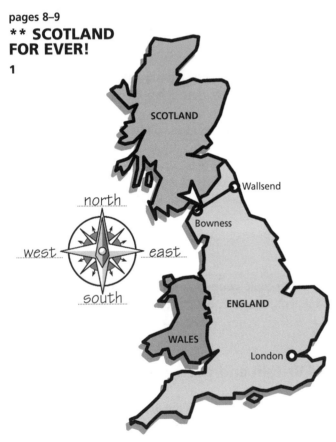

2 1 north 2 Wallsend 3 English 4 William Wallace
5 France 6 Elizabeth 7 King

3 One week.

4 1 The capital of Scotland is Edinburgh. 2 spider

5 2 unmarried 3 unlucky 4 impossible 5 unfriendly
6 incorrect

pages 10–11
*** THE IRISH QUESTION

1 1 b 2 a 3 a 4 b 5 b 6 a

2 2 republic 3 terrorist 4 Christians 5 independent

3 1 f 2 d 3 i 4 e 5 a 6 j 7 h 8 k 9 c 10 b 11 g

4 The Emerald Isle

5 2 get, got, got 3 be, was/were, been 4 leave, left, left
5 give, gave, given 6 go, went, gone
7 become, became, become 8 choose, chose, chosen

KINGS AND QUEENS

pages 12–13
* CRAZY KINGS

1 a Catherine of Aragon b Anne Boleyn c Jane Seymour
d Anne of Cleves e Catherine Howard f Katherine Parr

2 divorced, beheaded, died,
divorced, beheaded, survived.

3 He did a, b, c and d.

4 2 G 3 G 4 G 5 H 6 G 7 H 8 G 9 G 10 H 11 H 12 G

5 1 Tudor 2 Hanover

pages 14–15
** COOL QUEENS

1 1 Elizabeth 2 Victoria 3 Victoria 4 Elizabeth

2 2 cousin 3 wig 4 throne 5 the United Kingdom

3 2 E 3 V 4 E 5 V 6 V 7 E 8 E 9 V 10 V 11 E 12 V

4 Robert Dudley

5 2 the most popular 3 the largest 4 the thinnest
5 the greatest 6 the whitest 7 the fattest
8 the most famous 9 the reddest 10 the biggest

pages 16–17
*** ROMANTIC ROYALS

1 2 captain 3 navy 4 divorce 5 assassinate 6 royal
7 governor

2 Windsor

3 1 E 2 C 3 C 4 E 5 E 6 C

4 2 f 3 a 4 e 5 d 6 g 7 b 8 j 9 h 10 i

5 ABDICATION

HISTORIC BUILDINGS

pages 18–19
* THE QUEEN'S HOMES

1   2 lived 3 stays 4 started 5 had

2   1c 2d 3e 4b 5a

3   2 open 3 Royal 4 gardens 5 invites The dog is a CORGI.

4   ~~Victoria~~ Elizabeth, ~~1170s~~ 1070s, ~~1982~~ 1992, ~~small~~ big, ~~a hundred~~ five hundred, ~~blue~~ red, ~~coffee~~ tea

pages 20–21
** A PRISON AND A PALACE

1   2 bridge 3 prison 4 execute 5 crown 6 raven 7 maze 8 tennis 9 clock 10 moon

2   2 prison 3 executed 4 tower 5 crowns 6 ravens

3   2 the size of the moon 3 a vine 4 deer 5 A fire

4   2 Henry VIII lived there. (HC) 3 The guides are in Tudor clothes. (HC) 4 The Beefeaters got meat as pay (TOL) 5 They executed a lot of people there. (TOL) 6 Two young princes died there (TOL)

5   2 Crown Jewels 3 home 4 old 5 Cardinal Wolsey 6 guards

6   1 Edward 2 Richard

pages 22–23
*** TOP UNIVERSITIES: OXFORD AND CAMBRIDGE

1   1 False 2 True 3 True 4 True 5 False 6 False

2   2 The first students 3 No married teachers 4 Women students 5 An exciting competition 6 Staying at the universities

3   wearing boots curly hair near a house that sells wine

4   1 cap 2 gown 3 bow tie 4 ribbon 5 bicycle

6   Oxford: 1e 2d 3b 4a 5c Cambridge: 1c 2e 3b 4a 5d

FAMOUS EXPLORERS

pages 24–25
*SEA EXPLORERS

1   2d 3a 4c

2   2f 3a 4e 5h 6c 7b 8d

3   coconuts

4   2e 3b 4a 5d

5   1 TOBACCO 2 POTATOES

6   2 but 3 so 4 because 5 Then 6 or

pages 26–27
** EXTREME EXPLORERS

1   2 snow and ice 3 penguins and seals 4 fur 5 sledge 6 dogs 7 frostbite

2   2e 3d 4a 5c

3   2 pay 3 months 4 always 5 impossible

4   Open answers.

5   2 coldest 3 worst 4 as 5 best 6 better 7 as 8 bravest

6   The answer is at the bottom of page 27.

pages 28–29
*** EXPLORERS IN AFRICA

1   1 west coast 2 The Sahara Desert 3 The River Nile 4 Lake Victoria 5 east coast

2   1796-1805 = c 1854 = d 1856-1858 = b the 1860s = a

3   2 Park and Burton 3 Park 4 The Bakers 5 Burton 6 Burton

4   2 hated 3 shot 4 discovered 5 received 6 disappeared 7 became 8 carried

5   2 MEDAL 3 MAGGOT 4 DROWN 5 THERMOMETER

6   It's his heart.

FAMOUS WOMEN

pages 30–31
* FLORENCE NIGHTINGALE: THE LADY WITH THE LAMP

1   2a 3b 4e 5c

2   2 books 3 student 4 job 5 hospital 6 dirty 7 food 8 countries

3   2 must 3 mustn't 4 must 5 mustn't 6 must 7 mustn't 8 must 9 must 10 mustn't

4   2c 3g 4b 5d 6f 7h 8e
2   Florence was in bed for the last 14 years of her life.
3   Florence wrote letters to all the families of the dead soldiers.
4   International Nurses' Day is on Florence's birthday.
5   When Florence was in the Crimea, the doctors did not want to see her.
6   There is a Florence Nightingale Museum in Saint Thomas's Hospital in London.
7   Florence's aunt, Mai Smith, was also a nurse in the Crimea.
8   Three hospitals in Turkey have the name 'Florence Nightingale'.

pages 32–33
** ELIZABETH FRY: A LIFE OF GOOD WORK

1 b to sew c to hang d to steal e blanket f guard g cell

2 2 True 3 False (There were many women prisoners in each room.) 4 True 5 False (She was against hanging.) 6 True 7 False (Some of the Fry nurses went to the Crimea with Florence Nightingale.) 8 False (Queen Victoria gave Elizabeth money to help her.)

3 1 on 2 a 3 five 4 pound 6 note
Answer: On a five pound note.

4 2 boring 3 tired 4 exciting 5 interesting 6 bored 7 excited 8 tiring

pages 34–35
*** VOTES FOR WOMEN

1 Open answers.

2 2 1918 - women over 30, 1928 - women over 21 3 The suffragettes 4 They broke windows, destroyed pictures, and burned buildings. 5 a she was the leader of the suffagettes, b the British Prime Minister in 1908, c a suffragette who died at the Epsom Derby, d the first woman MP 6 They worked in offices, factories and farms.

3 2 kills 3 mouth 4 twelve 5 abroad

4 don't eat…'ll make 3 won't be…don't give 4 don't get…'ll jump 5 will never receive… act 6 goes…'ll be 7 'll die…don't eat 8 become…'ll get 9 will be…get 10 have to…'ll run

5 The Isle of Man

FAMOUS MEN

pages 36–37
* THEY CARED FOR POOR WORKERS

1 2 traders 3 lands 4 slaves 5 village 6 workers 7 factory 8 south

2 b slaves c traders d lands e factory f workers g south h village

3 2 ~~help~~ stop
3 ~~sugar~~ slaves
4 ~~after~~ before
5 ~~Hull~~ Birmingham
6 ~~sugar~~ chocolate
7 ~~didn't listen~~ listened
8 ~~dirty~~ clean

4 1 so 2 because

5 2 because 3 so 4 because 5 because 6 so

pages 38–39
** THEY HELPED YOUNG PEOPLE

1 1 a club for boys 2 In 1908 3 Because English boys liked Baden Powell's book on scouting for black African scouts. Because Baden Powell wanted to help young people. 4 Robert Baden Powell. 5 Over 76.

3 2 defended 3 war 4 chief 5 tracks 6 attacked 7 diamond 8 scouts

4 Afrikaans

5 2 Where did they send him? 3 Who did he work with there? 4 Which town did the Boers attack in 1900? 5 How many men did Baden Powell have? 6 How long did he defend the town? 7 When did he start the 'Boy Scouts'? 8 What did he become in 1929?

6 2 To South Africa 3 Black African scouts 4 Mafeking 5 1,251 (one thousand two hundred and fifty-one) 6 For 271 days 7 In 1908 8 Lord Baden Powell

7 2 F He was an unhappy child. 3 T 4 F He did a lot to help poor people. 5 F He stopped to children doing the poorest and dirtiest jobs. 6 T

pages 40–41
FAMOUS FIGHTERS

1 2 telescope 3 admiral 4 battle 5 captain 6 invade. 7 victory

2 Horatio

3 5 Battle of Trafalgar 2 Tenerife 3 Battle of the Nile 4 Battle of Copenhagen 6 Victory 7 Saint Paul's Cathedral 8 Lady Hamilton

4 A barrel of rum.
Culture Note: For this reason English people sometimes call rum 'Nelson's blood'!

5 2 Saint Helena 3 Waterloo 4 Russia 5 Portuguese…Spanish 6 Napoleon

6 1 boots 2 station

DREADFUL DISASTERS

pages 42–43
* THE GREAT FIRE OF LONDON

1 2b 3c 4b 5c

2 2 shouted 3 frightened 4 window 5 expensive 6 clothes

3 1 ph(o)tos 4 n(e)w 5 pho(n)e 9 ca(m)era 10 diar(y)

4 money

5 2 river 3 beautiful 4 quickly 5 churches 6 it

6 1 cheese 2 wine

pages 44–45
** THE BLACK DEATH

1

2 **Signs of the illness**: coughing up blood, swellings on the body, fever **Causes**: God was angry, touching an ill person, drinking bad water, rats, bad air **Treatment**: eating grass, taking blood from the ill person, killing cats and dogs, leaving the cities 1 The real cause was germs on fleas. The rats carried the fleas 2 The best treatment was to escape from the towns and cities.

4 2 in 1350 3 3 days 4 about half 5 'The Great Plague' 6 one third

pages 46–47
*** THE *TITANIC*

1 Edith Haisman was speaking after the accident.

2 2 practically 3 sink 4 crew 5 instantly
Opposites: float/sink

3 2 False (It hit an iceberg.) 3 True 4 True 5 False (More than two-thirds of the people died.)
6 False (The ship sank on its first and only voyage.)

4 **Order**: 1i 2g 3f 4j 5a 6d 7c 8h 9k 10b 11e

5 Southampton

THE WORST WARS

pages 48–49
* THE WARS OF THE ROSES

1 1 the rose must be white 2 the rose must be red

2 2 princes 3 cousin 4 marry 5 prison 6 uncle

3 2 Lord Warwick 3 Edward of York/Edward IV
4 Lord Warwick 5 Edward of York/Edward IV
6 Richard III 7 Henry Tudor/ Henry VII 8 Henry Tudor

4 2 Edward the Fourth 3 Edward the Fifth
4 Henry the Sixth 5 Henry the Seventh

5 2 – 3 – 4 a 5 The 6 a 7 an 8 the

pages 50–51
** THE ENGLISH CIVIL WAR

1 1 Charles II 2 Oliver Cromwell

2 2 republic 3 attack 4 forgive 5 army 6 betrayed

3 1 True 2 False (He often needed money.) 3 True
4 False (The Scots weren't happy with Charles.) 5 True
6 False (He became the leader of England, but not King.)
7 False (Richard Cromwell didn't pay the army.)
8 False (He didn't decide to forgive his father's killers.)

4 THEATRES

5 2 king 3 rich 4 expensive 5 bad 6 hate 7 closed
8 impossible 9 unhappy 10 little/not much 11 laughed

pages 52–53
*** TWO WORLD WARS

1 1 Your country needs YOU! (WW1) 2 Is your journey really necessary? (WW2) 3 Careless talk costs lives! (WW2)

2 2 nephew 3 poison 4 ally 5 Peace Treaty 6 curtains
7 agreement

3 2 WW2 3 WW1 4 WW1 5 WW2 6 WW2 7 WW2
8 WW1

4 EVACUEES

5 2 ended 3 Britain 4 wear 5 soldiers 6 flower

WONDERFUL WRITERS

pages 54–55
* THREE GREAT WRITERS

1 2 True 3 True 4 True 5 False (It was far away)
6 True (two on the way there and two on the way back)
7 True 8 False (Most of the stories are funny.)

2 1b 2a 3d 4c

3 2 Shakespeare 3 Dickens 4 Dickens 5 Shakespeare
6 Chaucer 7 Shakespeare 8 Chaucer

4 2 riding 3 writing 4 acting 5 sitting 6 standing
7 shouting 8 working 9 being 10 reading 11 seeing

5 Romeo and Juliet

pages 56–57

** WOMEN WRITERS

1 2 She wore jeans a lot. 3 Jane drove a red sports car.
4 She used a computer to write her novels.
5 She looked for one on the Internet.

2 2 George Henry Lewes 3 John Cross 4 Jane Austen

3 Charlotte Bronte = Currer Bell, Emily Bronte = Ellis Bell,
Anne Bronte = Acton Bell

4 1 George Eliot 2 Jane Austen 3 The Brontes
Note: *Agnes Grey* was by Anne; *Jane Eyre*, *Shirley*
and *Villette* were by Charlotte; *Wuthering Heights*
was by Emily.

5 1 know 2 drew 3 wrote 4 got 5 fell 6 worked
7 went 8 was

6 *Jane Eyre*

pages 58–59

*** ROMANTIC POETS

1 2 Keats 3 all of them 4 all of them 5 Wordsworth
6 Keats

2 b sung, tongue c page, age d wide, died e free, be
f how, allow g pen, ten

3 2 young 3 free 4 died 5 allow 6 pen

4 2 False (Byron, Shelley and Keats went to live in different
countries) 3 False (They wanted lots of people to read
their poetry.) 4 True 5 False (He had an opium
problem.) 6 True 7 False (He wrote about beautiful
things.) 8 True 9 False (He was a rebel when he was
young, but he didn't like change when he was older.)
10 False (It is very popular with tourists today.)

5 computer program

INVENTIONS, DISCOVERIES AND SCIENCE

pages 60–61

* THEY CHANGED THEIR WORLD

1 2 television 3 book 4 telephone 5 radio 6 printing press

2 2nd the printing press (1455 - Johann Gutenberg,
Germany), 3rd the telephone (1849 - Meucci/1876 - Bell),
4th radio (1893 - Marconi, Italy), 5th TV (1926 - Baird,
1927 - Philo Pharnsworth, USA), 6th computers (1941 -
first modern computer 'the Z3' - Konrad Zuse, Germany;
1943 first modern British computer 'Colossus' -
Tommy Flowers.)

3 2d 3e 4b 5a

4 2 False. Gutenberg was the first European to use a
printing press to make books. Caxton took the idea
to England. 3 True. He died before he could finish it.
4 False. Ada Lovelace wrote it. 5 False. He was Scottish,
and later American. 6 True. 7 False. The pictures were
very small. 8 True. People wanted to watch
the coronation.
NOTE Antonio Meucci, an Italian, made the world's
earliest telephone in 1849 in Cuba, but Bell's telephone
worked better.

5 TELECOMMUNICATIONS

pages 64–65

** THEY DISCOVERED IT

1 **Possible answers (probably many in L1):**
1 No, I haven't./Yes, I've had a cold, flu, measles, chicken
pox, mumps, etc. 2 No, I don't. They hurt. I'm scared.,
etc./Yes, I do. I don't like the dentist to hurt me., etc.
3 No, I haven't./Yes, when I cut / hurt my foot.
4 No, I've never been in hospital./Yes. When I broke
my leg. When I had a bad stomach., etc
5 No, I haven't. /Yes, when I had appendicitis., etc.

2 2 smallpox 3 vaccination 4 cow

3 1 True 2 False (Doctors wore ordinary clothes for
operating.) 3 True 4 False (Doctors didn't always
clean their knives.)

4 2 He used his computer to do this. 3 He told everyone
about it on TV the next day. 4 They used mobile phones
to talk to each other as they worked in different
laboratories. 5 They made the computer game 'Penicillin'
the next year.

5 2F 3J 4F 5L 6L 7J 8L

pages 64–65

*** GREAT THINKERS

1 2 theory 3 telescope 4 royal 5 evolution 6 mint
7 gravity

2 1 Newton 2 Darwin 3 Darwin 4 Newton

3 2 N 3 D 4 D 5 N 6 D 7 D 8 N 9 D 10 N)

4 1 THE ORIGIN OF SPECIES 2 THE PRINCIPIA

TRANSPORT

pages 66–67

* CARS

1 1b 2b 3a 4a 5b 6a

3 2 traffic lights 3 middle 4 horn 5 indicators
6 speed limit 7 fine 8 (traffic) accident

3 2 four 3 40th 4 1999 5 5,000 6 70,000 7 147

4 2 ~~behind~~ in front of 3 ~~warm~~ cold
4 ~~fewer~~ more 6 ~~right~~ left
7 ~~hate~~ love

pages 68–69
** TRAINS
1

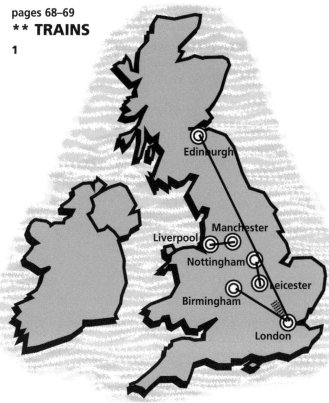

2 2d 3h 4a 5c 6b 7f 8e

3 TRAINSPOTTERS

4 2 chief 3 project 4 engineer 5 steam

5 2 job 3 money 4 built 5 hill 6 animals 7 slowly
8 through 9 son

pages 70–71
*** BOATS

1 2d 3e 4f 5b 6a

2 2 ~~Antarctic~~ Atlantic 3 ~~London~~ in Portsmouth
4 ~~India~~ China 5 ~~without stopping~~ stopping only once
6 ~~person~~ woman or ~~2001~~ 2005.

3 2 telegraph cable 3 trimaran 4 industries 5 transported
6 battle

4 Many canals* were built (during) the Industrial
Revolution* to transport things. Today, you can make
(trips) on a canal barge.

Towards the end of the 20th century, it became (cheaper)
to build ships abroad. Many British shipyards* closed.
Now many of the once-empty docklands* near the
(rivers) in Britain's cities have houses, offices, and
(restaurants) in them.

A popular British holiday is going on a cruise*.
You (sleep) on the boat and stop at different places.

The largest and most (expensive) passenger ship, or
liner*, in history is the Queen Mary II (or QM2 for short).
In January 2005, it celebrated its (first) year of making
trips from Britain to the USA.

5 2 yacht 3 liner 4 barge

MUSIC, ART, CRAFTS AND LEISURE

pages 72–73
* MARVELLOUS MUSICIANS

1 2 symphony 3 march 4 comic opera

2 1S 2E 3S 4E 5E 6S

3 As a boy Arthur Sullivan sang for Queen <u>Victoria</u> . He
studied music in <u>England and Germany</u>. The Queen <u>loved</u>
his music. Sullivan wrote <u>comic</u> operas with W.S. Gilbert.
One of them – The Mikado – was about the fashion for
<u>Japanese</u> things. He became Sir Arthur Sullivan in <u>1883</u>.
Edward Elgar came from a <u>poor</u> family. His father had a
<u>music</u> shop. Elgar married in 1889. After that his music
got <u>better</u>. His first great work was Enigma Variations. He
wrote <u>very little</u> music after his wife died.

4 1 PRINCESS 2 SORCERER 3 PIRATES

pages 74–75
** CLEVER CRAFTSMEN

2 ARCHITECT
3 DESIGNER
4 POLITICIAN
5 CRAFTWORKER
6 PAINTER
7 BUSINESSMAN
8 PUBLISHER
9 POET

2 Josiah Wedgwood: potter, craftworker, businessman
William Morris: architect, painter, designer, craftworker,
poet, politician, publisher

3 2 M 3 W 4 W 5 M 6 M 7 W 8 M 9 W 10 M

4 1 Charlotte 2 wallpaper

pages 76–77
*** JOSEPH PAXTON AND THE
CRYSTAL PALACE

1 invest 2 iron 3 prince 4 exhibition 5 model 6 empire
7 dinosaurs 8 crystal

2 VICTORIA

3 1a 2b 3b

4 2 ~~airports~~ railways 3 ~~poor~~ rich 4 ~~magazine~~ newspaper
5 ~~Edward~~ Albert, ~~son~~ husband 6 ~~Science~~ Victoria and
Albert Museum 7 ~~North~~ South 8 ~~1963~~ 1936.

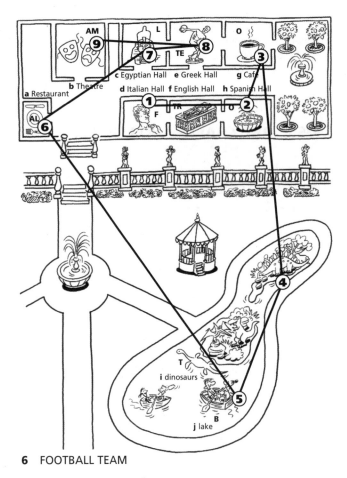

a Restaurant
b Theatre
c Egyptian Hall   **e** Greek Hall   **g** Café
d Italian Hall   **f** English Hall   **h** Spanish Hall
i dinosaurs
j lake
T
B
TR
F
AL
AM
L
TE
O

6   FOOTBALL TEAM

BRITAIN AND THE WORLD

pages 78–79
* NORTH AMERICA

1   1 furs 2 factory 3 tobacco 4 queen 5 potatoes
6 farmers

2   2 False (They started a new town, Plymouth in the USA.
It gets its name from Plymouth in England – they sailed
from there.), 3 True, 4 False (It lost them between 1775
and 1781), 5 True, 6 True

3   2 someone 3 Everyone 4 no one 5 someone 6 everyone

4   2 Pilgrim Fathers 3 Mayflower 4 Plymouth 5 Scotland

M	T	E	A	O	A	Z	Y	N	A	T	S	L	A
P	I	L	G	R	I	M	F	A	T	H	E	R	S
L	N	S	F	X	H	A	S	T	D	S	O	E	C
Y	Y	E	E	W	E	Y	D	A	G	E	E	X	O
M	S	T	E	K	D	F	R	T	N	H	Y	S	T
O	A	S	L	D	A	L	A	Y	S	A	G	H	L
U	E	R	T	F	R	O	M	T	E	W	M	O	A
T	Y	T	M	P	D	W	T	D	L	E	D	D	N
H	Y	S	S	Y	N	E	N	W	E	E	D	A	D
O	A	Y	D	V	I	R	G	I	N	I	A	T	E

pages 80–81
** AUSTRALIA AND NEW ZEALAND

1   b5 c2 d7 e1 f6 g4

2   1 convicts 2 big 3 farms 4 rich 5 in 1901 6 with

3   2 unlucky 3 unfair 4 impossible 5 uncomfortable
6 unfriendly 7 unkind 8 disappeared 9 unhappy
10 unusual 11 unreal

4   2g 3a 4f 5i 6j 7h 8b 9e 10d

5   Wellington

pages 82–83
*** INDIA

1   1b 2a 3b 4a 5b 6b

2   2 spices 3 republic 4 non-violent 5 Crown 6 silk

3   1d 2g 3c 4i 5e 6b 7f 8a 9h

4   Bollywood (Bombay + Hollywood)

5   1 'curry' (from Tamil, a language of south-east
India and Sri Lanka)
2 'pyjamas' (from Urdu, the Indian language spoken
in the south of India)
3 'bungalow' (from Hindi, the language spoken in
northern and central India)
NOTE: 23 languages are spoken in Indian -
including English!

QUIZZES

QUIZ 1

A: 1c 2b 3a; B: 1c 2a 3b; C: 1a 2b 3a; D: 1b 2c 3b;
E: 1b 2c 3c; F: 1a 2c 3b; G: 1b 2c 3b; H: 1c 2b 3a;
I: 1c 2c 3b; J: 1c 2b 3b; K: 1c 2a 3c;
L:1b 2c 3b; M: 1b 2c 3b

QUIZ 2

A: 1c 2b 3c; B: 1a 2c 3c; C: 1b 2c 3b; D: 1c 2a 3b;
E: 1a 2b 3b; F: 1b 2a 3c; G: 1c 2b 3b; H: 1b 2c 3c;
I: 1c 2b 3a; J: 1a 2c 3b; K: 1c 2c 3b;
L: 1b 2c 3b; M: 1c 2b 3a

QUIZ 3

A: 1c 2b 3c; B: 1a 2c 3c; C: 1b 2c 3c; D: 1c 2a 3b;
E: 1b 2c 3b; F: 1b 2a 3b; G: 1c 2b 3a; H: 1c 2b 3c;
I: 1b 2a 3c; J: 1a 2c 3b; K: 1b 2c 3a;
L: 1b 2b 3c; M: 1a 2c 3b